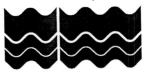

# PEVSNER'S
# ARCHITECTURAL GLOSSARY

Nikolaus and Lola Pevsner, Hampton Court,
in the gardens by Wren's east front, probably *c.* 1960

# PEVSNER'S
# ARCHITECTURAL
# GLOSSARY

Yale University Press
New Haven and London

YALE UNIVERSITY PRESS
NEW HAVEN AND LONDON
302 Temple Street, New Haven CT 06511
47 Bedford Square, London WC1B 3DP
www.pevsner.co.uk
www.lookingatbuildings.org.uk
www.yalebooks.co.uk
www.yalebooks.com
for
THE PEVSNER BOOKS TRUST


Published by Yale University Press 2010
2 4 6 8 10 9 7 5 3 1


ISBN 978 0 300 16721 4


Copyright © Yale University, 2010


Printed by T. J. International, Padstow
Set in Monotype Plantin

# CONTENTS

## FOREWORD

The first volumes of Nikolaus Pevsner's Buildings of England series appeared in 1951. The intention was to make available, county by county, a comprehensive guide to the notable architecture of every period from prehistory to the present day. Building types, details and other features that would not necessarily be familiar to the general reader were explained in a compact glossary, which in the first editions extended to some 350 terms. As the English series progressed this figure grew considerably, and the advent in the 1970s of Scottish, Welsh and Irish volumes further multiplied the total. Fresh illustrations were commissioned too, culminating in 1995 in a completely new sequence of comparative drawings. These were supplied by the late John Sambrook, an exceptionally talented draughtsman who had worked for the Historic Buildings Division of the Greater London Council before making himself the foremost British expert on the history and construction of fanlights. It is these drawings which illustrate the text of the present book, which brings together for the first time in one volume the full and revised array of architectural terms from the English, Irish, Scottish and Welsh series.

One celebrated feature of the first series was the use of the abbreviations E.E., Dec and Perp (Early English, Decorated, Perpendicular) for the successive phases of English Gothic. These originated in 1817 with Thomas Rickman's *An Attempt to Discriminate the Styles of English Architecture from the Conquest to the Reformation*, and were given currency for later generations by Murray's Guides and by Methuen & Co.'s Little Guides, both of which were among Pevsner's habitual sources for his own fieldwork. For later styles of architecture, however, the books were silent. This omission was made good with the launch in 2000 of the website www.lookingatbuildings.org, funded by the Heritage Lottery Fund and compiled on behalf of the series'

research charity the Buildings Books Trust (now Pevsner
Books Trust), in which the greater space available on-line
made possible a more expansive definition of such terms as
Baroque, Rococo, Neoclassical and Art Deco than has ever
been feasible in the individual Buildings glossaries. These
terms now take their place in the present book,
together with photographic illustrations of key examples. The
whole is at once a reference work in its own right, and a
companion and supplement to the four nations of the
Pevsner Architectural Guides series.

Simon Bradley

# ROUNDELS

The roundels which mark the opening of each alphabetical section appeared on the covers of paperback editions of the series produced between 1951 and 1964. Each is based on an illustration reproduced in the volume, and the majority were drawn by the designer Berthold Wolpe. Exceptions are *Cornwall*, by Andrea Lee; *Herefordshire*, *Wiltshire*, and *Lincolnshire* by Fred Price; and *London except...* by the London County Council Architects' Office.

# FIGURES

# PLATES

The colour plates are divided into three chronological sections: Ecclesiastical (after p. 32), Public, and Domestic (after
p. 80), the sequence used in the county gazetteers. In this
list captions are followed by an excerpt from the description,
with its page reference, from the relevant volume. The text
has been lightly edited in some cases. Each entry starts with a
stylistic definition in italic, and within the text terms explained
in the glossary are also in italic. A complete list of all the
Pevsner Architectural Guides in print appears on p. 140.

## ECCLESIASTICAL

1  *Anglo-Saxon*: Colchester, Holy Trinity, w doorway. ESSEX,
   p. 264.
   'The tower is built with plenty of Roman bricks. Its small
   w doorway with triangular head a wholly *Anglo-Saxon*
   feature.'

2  *Norman*: Edstaston, St Mary, s doorway of nave, late C12.
   SHROPSHIRE, p. 260.
   'The nave s doorway is extremely sumptuous. Four orders
   of *shafts* plus demi-shafts in the *jambs*. *Leaf capitals*. The
   *orders* of the *arch* have a variety of *chevron* and *crenellation*
   motifs. The *hoodmould*, starting from *headstops*, shares
   these motifs. A head also at its apex.'

3  *Norman*: Waltham Abbey, Holy Cross and St Lawrence,
   second quarter of the C12. ESSEX, p. 808.
   'The *Norman* nave has something of the sturdy force of
   Durham Cathedral. The *elevation*, as in most major
   Anglo-Norman churches, is of *arcade*, *gallery* and
   *clerestory*. The *arcades* have supports alternating between
   *composite piers* and subordinate round ones. The *composite
   piers* have a *buttress*-like broad flat projection to the nave
   with demi-shaft attached running up to the ceiling without any break apart from the clerestory *sill*. The
   *capitals* are big and heavy, single- or double-*scalloped*.'

9 Worcester Cathedral, misericord, jousting scene, *c.* 1397. WORCESTERSHIRE, p. 689.
'A fine set of *misericords* from the stalls of 1379. Thirty-seven complete scenes, all with supporters.'

10 *Perpendicular / Tudor*: Sefton, St Helen, parclose screen, early C16. LANCASHIRE: LIVERPOOL AND THE SOUTH-WEST, p. 581.
'exquisitely fine late *Gothic tracery*.'

11 *Decorated*: Pershore Abbey, chancel vault, probably *c.* 1290–1300. WORCESTERSHIRE, p. 528.
'It consists of *transverse arches*, diagonal *ribs*, ridge *ribs*, one pair of *tiercerons* to N and S, but in addition *lierne* ribs (possibly their first surviving usage), forming a kind of scissors movement: open-closed-open-closed, all along.'

12 *Perpendicular / Tudor*: Gestingthorpe, St Mary, double-hammerbeam roof attributed to Thomas Loveday, *c.* 1525. ESSEX, p. 376.
'uncommonly splendid for Essex, it is of the double-*hammerbeam* type of which there are only a few in the county.'

13 *Perpendicular / Tudor*: Westminster Abbey, Chapel of Henry VII, *c.* 1503–12, vault, attributed to William Vertue. LONDON 6: WESTMINSTER, p. 137.
'A *fan vault* of the most glorious richness and size, of the kind known as a *pendant* fan vault... The division into bays is by strong *transverse arches* with a fringe of *cusping*. These are given a form similar to the *arched braces* of timber roofs. Thence also comes the openwork *tracery* in their spandrels, here combined with a diagonal bracing rib... The points are marked by huge pendants, from which the greater area of the fans themselves radiate.'

14 *Baroque / Artisan Mannerist*: Minsterley, Holy Trinity, by William Taylor, 1688–9, W front. SHROPSHIRE, p. 407.
'The oddest facade, rich with sculpture. *Rusticated giant* pilasters support an open segmental *pediment*. Within this frame the most elaborate feature is the W portal. It has rustication l. and r., an exaggeratedly eared frame and a *segmental frieze* and *cornice*. The *keystone* is carved with the usual cherub's head and there are flanking reliefs of skulls and bones in the frieze... Above all this is an arched window with radiating *voussoirs* and cherub keystone. Garlands hang down the flanking *pilasters*.'

15  *Baroque*: Christ Church, Spitalfields, 1714–29, by
    Nicholas Hawksmoor, west front. LONDON 5: EAST,
    p. 389.
    'The most overpowering of Hawksmoor's three great
    *Baroque* churches of the East End. The w tower rises be-
    hind the oddest of *porticoes*. It consists of four *Tuscan
    columns*, the outer ones carrying a straight *entablature*, the
    inner ones a semicircular *arch*... The tower is even
    stranger. Seen from the w, the effect is of a *triumphal arch*
    raised up on high, with the central opening breaking
    through a heavy *cornice* flanked by arched *niches*.'

16  *Gothic Revival / Gothick*: Croome D'Abitot, St Mary
    Magdalene, 1759–63, almost certainly by Lancelot Brown.
    WORCESTERSHIRE, p. 242.
    'As built it is medievalizing: one of the most serious of the
    early *Gothic Revival* outside, one of the most elegant
    within.'

17  *Neo-classical*: Shrewsbury, St Chad, by George Steuart,
    1790–2. SHROPSHIRE, p. 523.
    'an original and distinguished design, indeed one of the
    finest *Neo-classical* churches in Britain... a circular body,
    prefaced by a mighty tower with a *portico*, *vestries* l. and r.
    and an *apse*-ended link for the *gallery* stairs.'

18  *Gothic Revival / Gothick*: St George, Heyworth Street,
    Everton, built by John Cragg, 1813–14. LIVERPOOL CITY
    GUIDE, p. 265.
    'extraordinarily light and delicate due to the use of *cast
    iron* throughout. Slender clustered *columns* divide *nave*
    from *aisles*. Traceried *arches* span between the columns to
    support the nave ceiling, and between the columns and
    the outer wall to carry the flat ceilings over the aisles (the
    tie-rods are a C20 insertion).'

19  *Gothic Revival*: Alvechurch, St Laurence, 1857–61, by
    William Butterfield. WORCESTERSHIRE, p.106.
    'One of the best of Butterfield's surviving brick colour
    schemes... The *nave* walls are patterned with crisp white
    *diaper* against glowing red brick, but subservient to the
    white stone bands dominating the forceful *clerestory*.
    *Arcades* of alternating buff and pink sandstone.'

20  *Gothic Revival*: Interior view of St Michael's and All An-
    gels Church, nave by William Burges, 1893–5. BRIGHTON
    AND HOVE CITY GUIDE, p. 50.

'C13 in style and cathedral-like, it has a *triforium* and a
*clerestory* tied to the *arcades* below by shafting running up
beside the piers, clustered *shafting* to the upper parts and
detached inner *arcading* to the triforium which repeats the
*tracery*.'

21 *Neo-Byzantine*: Bradford, Heaton, Our Lady and the First
Martyrs, by J.H. Langtry-Langton, 1935, interior. YORK-
SHIRE WEST RIDING: LEEDS, BRADFORD AND THE NORTH,
p. 178.
'The first church in England designed with a central
altar... Octagonal, with a central *lantern* stage carried on
a series of radiating semi parabolic beams spanning the
interior.'

22 *Modernist*: St Paul, Bow Common, by Maguire & Murray,
1956–60, interior. LONDON 5: EAST, p. 607.
'lit from above and defined by the slender white *columns*
dividing [the centre] from the surrounding triangular-
vaulted *aisles*. The altar is raised on steps, emphasized by
the hanging steel *corona* and *baldacchino*.'

PUBLIC BUILDINGS

23 *Norman*: Castle Hedingham, the keep, *c.* 1142. ESSEX,
p. 193.
'Built by one of the most powerful families of Norman
England. It stands to this day as an ideal picture of a *keep*
– on a mount, high above old trees, with two of its square
corner turrets still rising up to nearly 100 ft. It is, more-
over, probably the best preserved of all tower-keeps of
England.'

24 *Perpendicular*: Manchester, Chetham's School and
Library, cloister, 1420s. LANCASHIRE: MANCHESTER
AND THE SOUTH-EAST, pp. 294–6.
'The buildings are of red sandstone with a stone flag
roof... The *cloister* has a walk around a garth with three-
light openings to three sides... Stepped *buttresses* divide
the *bays*. Lower windows have *cinquefoil* heads, upper
windows in alternate bays only, *trefoil* heads.'

25 *Timber framing*: Thaxted, Guildhall, third quarter of the
C15, altered in 1715 and by Ernest Beckwith in 1910–11.
ESSEX, p. 766.

'Three-storeyed, free-standing on three sides, and on
each of those three sides are not one but two *jetties*...
The ground floor is open, with simple *arches* between
the *posts*... the arches on the first floor are Beckwith's,
allegedly based on a single example that he found, while
the second-floor *oriels* are entirely conjectural.'

26   *Tudor*: Beamsley Hospital, founded 1593. YORKSHIRE WEST
RIDING: LEEDS, BRADFORD AND THE NORTH, p. 115.
'Circular, with a circular core carried up as a *lantern*. This
part is a chapel, the rooms encircling it *ambulatory*-wise
and mostly opening off it. Three chimney-stacks disposed
round the lantern, *mullioned* windows, conical roof with
*finial*.'

27   *Baroque*: Abingdon, County Hall, 1678–83, builder
Christopher Kempster. BERKSHIRE, p. 103.
'Of the free-standing town halls of England with open
ground floors this is the grandest. It is also remarkably
high and monumental for its two *storeys*. Tawny stone,
four by two *bays*. *Giant Composite pilasters* on very high
*plinths* used consistently. Open arches below, the windows
above of three *lights* arched with a *transom*, and the *mullions* forming a concentric arch above the transom.'

28   *Baroque*: Stydd, almshouses, s front, 1728. LANCASHIRE:
NORTH, p. 661.
'Very curious and very engaging. Five *bays*. The three middle
bays have on the first floor an *arcade* of *rustic Tuscan* columns
with *balustrading* to the outer bays. The *loggia* is reached by
an open staircase with curved sides. Truncated shaped *gable*
on top.'

29   *Italianate*: Perth, St John Street, Nos. 48–50 (former Central
Bank of Scotland, by David Rhind. 1846–7. PERTH AND
KINROSS, p. 631.
'Three-storey five-bay *palazzo*, with *rusticated quoins*. At the
ends of the ground floor, Roman *Doric pilastered* doorpieces
with *triglyphed friezes*. The *bases* of the inner pilasters are
linked by a *balustrade* under the *corniced* ground floor
windows. *Aedicular* first-floor windows.'

30   *Classical*: St George's Hall, the Concert Hall, 1850. LIVER-
POOL CITY GUIDE, p. 54.
'one of the greatest Victorian interiors, and perhaps more ex-
pressive of C19 civic pride and aspiration than any other. It is
roofed with a mighty *tunnel vault* which is carried on *columns*

of polished red granite, placed in front of massive *piers*, and there are *arches* between the piers. The Minton tile floor with its pattern of interlocking circles against a *diapered* background is by Cockerell.

31  *Classical*: Leeds Town Hall, Headrow, by Cuthbert Brodrick, 1852–8. LEEDS CITY GUIDE, pp. 63–4.
'The monumental flight of steps leading to the s front is an impressive prelude to the great ten-column *Corinthian colonnade*... There are pavilions to l. and r. with Corinthian columns between coupled *pilasters* and arched windows in two storeys. Above the s colonnade is the proud tower... with a detached square colonnade of six columns and a big, tall, rather elongated square lead-covered *dome* with concave sides crowned by a *cupola*.'

32  *Gothic Revival*: Liverpool, Victoria Building, University of Liverpool, by Alfred Waterhouse, 1889–92. LANCASHIRE: LIVERPOOL AND THE SOUTH-WEST, p. 363.
'To the l., the former library with *gabled dormers*; to the r., the principal staircase and a semi-circular lecture theatre, both expressed externally. Double height apsidal entrance hall faced in Burmantofts terracotta, glazed and unglazed, mostly browns with touches of pale blue.'

33  *Modernist / Art Deco*: Morecambe, Midland Hotel, by Oliver Hill, 1932–3, E side. LANCASHIRE: NORTH, p. 461.
'the first hotel of its type in England, in a style which evokes the *Modern Movement* without really being *Modernist*, yet seeming too substantial to be called merely *Art Deco*.'

34  *Modernist*: The Economist Group, St James's Street, London, 1962–4 by Alison and Peter Smithson. LONDON 6: WESTMINSTER, p. 636.
'The three towers are set on a *podium*, grouped and proportioned to suit the context – a radical departure at a time when *Modernist* practice was still dominated by stand-alone monumentalism. The towers have even *concrete* frames, with the corners *canted* to increase the amount of light.'

35  *Postmodernist*: Storm Water Pumping Station, Isle of Dogs, 1987–8 by John Outram. LONDON 5: EAST, p. 683.
'A primitive classical temple, *Postmodern* in its symbolism, classicism and vivid colour, inside and out, but in no way routine.'

36 *Modernist (High Tech)*: Sage Music Centre, Oakwellgate, Gateshead, 1996–2004, from the north-west. NEWCASTLE AND GATESHEAD CITY GUIDE, p. 91.
'The intricate roof has a maximum span of 260 ft (80 metres) formed by four primary *arches*, with beam segments of successively increasing radius giving a spiral profile. The result is a sheath undulating across a large strutted structure and wrapping round two small and one large *reinforced-concrete* halls.'

## DOMESTIC BUILDINGS

37 *Decorated*: Markenfield Hall, hall block, *c.* 1290–1310. YORKSHIRE WEST RIDING: LEEDS, BRADFORD AND THE NORTH, p. 585.
'L-shaped hall block at the NE corner of the courtyard – the principal element, taller than the rest – former lodgings range along the rest of the E side, former kitchen block W of the hall... The main rooms of the hall block are all on the upper floor, above a *undercroft* which was originally *vaulted* throughout. The *crenellated parapet*, originally with a wall-walk behind, is all of a piece.'

38 *Perpendicular*: Much Wenlock, Wenlock Priory, prior's lodging range from the W, late 1420s, wall perhaps rebuilt *c.* 1500. SHROPSHIRE, p. 425.
'the range is faced by two storeys of *galleries*, originally unglazed, like *cloister* walks, entered through an inconspicuous doorway at the N end. The galleries form a continuous grid of windows, very much as in a building of the C20. *Buttresses* between each pair of two-*light* openings. *Four-centred arches*. The whole impresses one as stately and yet entirely domestic.'

39 *Timber framed*: Bramley, Manor House, exterior, *c.* 1545–6. HAMPSHIRE: WINCHESTER AND THE NORTH, p. 195. '*timber-framed* with an impressive display of *close studding* to both floors. Restored by Thomas Stopher *c.* 1884–5. His are the diamond-leaded *oriel* windows, the star chimneys and scallop *tile-hanging*.'

40 *Elizabethan*: Fountains Hall, attributed to Robert Smythson, *c.* 1600. YORKSHIRE WEST RIDING: LEEDS, BRADFORD AND THE NORTH, p. 268.
'Round-headed doorway flanked by coupled *fluted Ionic columns* carrying an *entablature*... *Mullion-and-transom*

windows of five lights to l. and r., with mullioned basement windows below. On top of the *fore-building* is a
*balustrade*... then comes the spectacular *fenestration* of the
great chamber, a virtual 'glass wall' with a tall semicircular double-transomed *oriel* of five lights in the centre.'

41 *Palladian*: Hagley Hall, by Sanderson Miller, 1754–60.
WORCESTERSHIRE, p. 336.
'basement of even *ashlar rustication*. *Piano nobile* above
with windows with blind *balustrades*, then a half-storey
with square windows: the corner pavilions have an additional storey and windows emphasized with *pediments* or
ears. *Moulded cornice* with *balustraded parapet*.'

42 *Rococo*: Lytham Hall, staircase hall, plasterwork by
Guiseppe Cortese, *c*. 1764. LANCASHIRE: NORTH, p. 437.
'a rich *coffered* and *coved* ceiling, with everything presided
over by Zeus wielding thunderbolts as he treads billowing
clouds.'

43 *Neo-classical (Adam)*: Harewood House, Music Room, by
Robert Adam, *c*. 1765–71. YORKSHIRE WEST RIDING: LEEDS,
BRADFORD AND THE NORTH, p. 302.
'*Adam*'s decoration of the rooms was one of his largest
schemes, executed by many of his usual contacts... circular insets to the ceiling attributed to Biaggio Rebecca, a
wall scheme of large paintings of classical ruins by Anto-
nio Zucchi, and an Axminster carpet echoing the ceiling
design.'

44 *Pictureque / Regency*: Cronkhill, by John Nash, *c*. 1802–7.
SHROPSHIRE, p. 240.
'The earliest *Italiante* villa in England, of a new Picturesque sort which would become hugely popular throughout the first half of the C19. The design appears completely
informal, with a big round tower at one corner of the
main, two-storey block and a balustraded loggia to the l.'

45 *Gothic Revival / Regency*: Liverpool (Mossley Hill), Green-
bank, S front, *c*. 1812–16. LANCASHIRE: LIVERPOOL AND THE
SOUTH-WEST, p. 442.
'delightful *gothick*... on the S front is the most charming
two-storey iron veranda of delicate *tracery* across all four
*bays*.'

46 *Greek Revival*: The Grange, portico by William Wilkins,
*c*. 1809–10. HAMPSHIRE: WINCHESTER AND THE NORTH,
p. 297.

'At the E end Wilkins added the magnificent pedimented Doric portico, its order based on that of the Thesion in Athens. Everything is bigger and better than the contemporary portico at Stratton Park: it is *hexastyle* rather than *tetrastyle*, the *columns* are *fluted* rather than plain, and it is two columns deep… The whole is tied together by the *entablature* of *triglyphs* and *metope* wreaths.'

47 *Picturesque*: East Stratton, model estate cottages, by George Dance the Younger, 1806. HAMPSHIRE: WINCHESTER AND THE NORTH, p. 248.
'five pairs of model estate cottages with thatched roofs, Yorkshire sashes and *lean-to* porches.'

48 *Old English / Queen Anne*: Chigwell Hall, by Norman Shaw, 1875–6. ESSEX, p. 230.
'Brick ground floor, projecting *tile-hung* upper floor, and coved *eaves*. The S front has an asymmetrical *bay window*, three slightly projecting windows on the first floor and then three more windows in the broad *gables* above. The entrance is at the side, with a flat wooden hood over the doorway.'

49 *Arts and Crafts*: Castlemorton, Bannut Tree House, 1890, by C. F. A. Voysey. WORCESTERSHIRE, p. 216.
'Four even *gables* with *half-timbering*, a motif Voysey later more or less discarded. The upper floor is *jettied* out, though this is disguised by the picturesquely detailed chimney, l., by typically sloping *buttresses*, by the projecting garden porch, and also by the nice solution of the r. corner, where the ground-floor window bay is polygonal but the floor above juts out at a right angle.'

50 *Scottish Baronial*: Dall House, by Mackenzie & Matthews, 1854–5. PERTH AND KINROSS, p. 310.
'*Scottish Baronial* but lighthearted in its display of *crow-stepped gables*, round towers and turrets with witches'-hat roofs, and steeply *pedimented dormer heads*… the entrance contained in a bowed tower topped by a rectangular *cap-house*.'

51 *Arts and Crafts*: Sulhamstead, Folly Farm, by Sir Edwin Lutyens, 1905–12. BERKSHIRE, p. 539.
'Lutyens's original addition appears at first to be a complete, though relatively modest, '*Wrenaissance*' house looking out onto a formal canal and attached to the S end of the old farmhouse. Grey brick with *dressings* of unortho-

dox two-inch red bricks, raised *quoins*, hipped roof. Central full-height hall and two-storeyed wings.'

52  *Modernist*: Ulting, The Studio, by Richard & Su Rogers, 1968–9. ESSEX, p. 796.
'One of two executed experiments by Rogers for a steel-framed structure, built as far as possible with factory-made components: the width of the building is determined by the width of the available sheeting for the roof. In theory, the house was a prototype for a system that was capable of mass production.'

53  *Modernist*: Nolton, Malator, by Future Systems, 1998. PEMBROKESHIRE, p. 327.
'The seaward *elevation* is entirely of glass. Open plan with central living area, the kitchen and bathroom towards each end, these rooms within free-standing pear-shaped pods. Steel-framed construction, the roof supported on a steel ring-beam.'

## PHOTOGRAPHIC ACKNOWLEDGEMENTS

The publishers gratefully acknowledge the support of English Heritage and the Royal Commissions for Scotland and Wales. Their photographers have provided the majority of the images for the Pevsner Architectural Guides for a number of years. The images used in this book come from a variety of sources and are all taken from previous volumes in the series; they are acknowledged below.

Martin Charles: 30, 51
Chetham's Library: 24
English Heritage (NMR): 18, 31
English Heritage (Photo Library): 1, 2, 3, 4, 5, 6, 7, 9, 10, 11, 12, 14, 15, 16, 17, 19, 20, 21, 22, 23, 25, 26, 28, 32, 33, 34, 36, 37, 38, 39, 41, 42, 43, 44, 45, 46, 47, 48, 49, 52
The Dean and Chapter of Westminster: 13
Angelo Hornak: 27
National Trust Photographic Library/Andrew Butler: 40
John Outram: 35
Royal Commission on the Ancient and Historical Monuments of Scotland (RCAHMS, Crown Copyright): 29, 50
Royal Commission on the Ancient and Historical Monuments of Wales (RCAHMW, Crown Copyright): 8, 53

# NOTE TO THE READER

Numbers in square brackets refer to text figures and Plate numbers refer to the colour sections.

Captions for the plate sections are listed on pp. 9–19, with extracts from the original description in the Pevsner Architectural Guides. Terms defined in the Glossary are set in *italics*.

Literal meanings, where specially relevant, are indicated by the abbreviation *lit.*

The majority of the original drawings for the text figures are by John Sambrook.

**ABACUS**  Flat slab forming the top of a *capital* on a *column* or *pilaster* [23].

**ABUTMENT**  The meeting of an *arch* or *vault* with its solid lateral support, or the support itself.

**ACANTHUS**  *Classical* formalized leaf *ornament* [1].

Fig. 1  Acanthus

**ACCUMULATOR TOWER**  A tower housing a hydraulic accumulator which accommodates fluctuations in the flow through *hydraulic power* mains.

**ACHIEVEMENT**  In heraldry, a complete display of armorial bearings.

**ACROTERION** (plural: acroteria)  *Plinth* for a statue or *ornament* on the apex or ends of a *pediment*; more usually, both the plinth and what stands on it [27].

**ADAM**  A style associated with the Scottish architect Robert Adam (1728–92), marked by delicate all-over *ornament* derived largely from the decoration of ancient

*Roman* interiors. It is one of the major contributions to the *Neo-Classical* phase of British architecture [pl. 43].

**ADDORSED**  Descriptive of two figures placed back to back. Compare *affronted*.

**AEDICULE**  (*lit.* little building): Architectural surround, consisting usually of two *columns* or *pilasters* supporting a *pediment*.

**AESTHETIC MOVEMENT**  A late-19th-century approach to design, seen at its strongest in interiors and furniture, which rejected the moral fervour behind the *Gothic Revival* in favour of 'art for art's sake'. The results were often eclectic, drawing typically on *Renaissance, Oriental* and *ancient Greek* sources. It overlapped with the early *Arts and Crafts* movement and the *Queen Anne* style.

**AFFRONTED**  Descriptive of two figures placed front to front. Compare *addorsed*.

**AGGREGATE**  Small stones or rock chippings used in *concrete* and similar hard-setting materials.

**AISLE**  Subsidiary space alongside the body of a building, separated from it by *columns, piers* or *posts*. Also (especially Scots) projecting wing of a church, often for special use, e.g. by a guild or by a landed family whose burial place it may contain.

**ALMONRY**  A building from which alms are dispensed to the poor.

**ALTARPIECE**  A painting or carving above or behind an altar.

**AMBO**  Raised platform or *pulpit* in *Early Christian* churches.

**AMBULATORY**  (*lit.* walkway): *Aisle* around the *sanctuary* of a church.

**ANGLE BUTTRESS**  A *buttress* set at 90 degrees at the angle of a building. Effectively, a continuation of the wall beyond the enclosure [7].

**ANGLE ROLL**  *Roll moulding* in the angle between two planes [13].

**ANGLE ROUND**  (Scots): A rounded *bartizan* or *turret*, usually roofless, set at a corner [35].

**ANGLE VOLUTE**  A pair of *volutes* or spiral *scrolls* turned outwards to meet at the corner of a *capital*, especially an *Ionic* capital.

**ANGLO-SAXON**  The architecture of the 7th to mid-11th centuries, i.e. before the Norman Conquest of 1066. There are no known secular survivals, but Saxon churches are distinguished from those of the Continent by certain masonry techniques such as *long-and-short work* (qv) [pl. 1]. See also *Saxo-Norman*.

**ANNULET**  A ring around a circular *pier* or a *shaft* attached to a pier, typical of the 12th and 13th centuries. Also called a *shaft-ring*.

**ANSE DE PANIER**  (French, *lit.* basket handle): *Arch* of three-centred and depressed type, or with a flat centre; also called a *basket arch*.

**ANTAE** (singular: anta)  Simplified *pilasters*, usually applied to the ends of the side walls of a *classical* building. When these side walls are extended to the front of a *portico*, it is said to be *in antism* [27].

**ANTEFIXAE**  *Ornaments* projecting at regular intervals above a Greek *cornice*, originally to conceal the ends of roof tiles [27].

**ANTHEMION**  *Classical ornament* like a honeysuckle flower [2].

Fig. 2   Anthemion and palmette

**APRON**  Raised panel below a window or *wall monument* or *tablet*.

**APSE**  Semicircular or polygonal end of an apartment, especially of a *chancel* or *chapel*. In *classical* architecture sometimes called an *exedra*.

**ARABESQUE**  Non-figurative surface decoration consisting of flowing lines, foliage *scrolls* etc., based on geometrical patterns. Compare *grotesque*.

**ARCADE**  Series of *arches* supported by *piers* or *columns* (compare *colonnade*). **BLIND ARCADE OR ARCADING**: the same applied to the wall surface. **WALL ARCADE**: in medieval churches, a *blind arcade* forming a *dado* below windows. Also a covered shopping street.

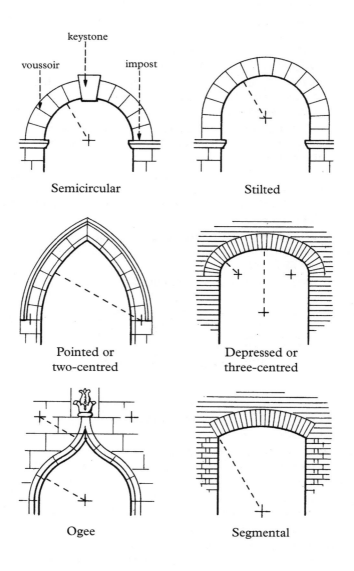

keystone

voussoir          impost

Semicircular                    Stilted

Pointed or                      Depressed or
two-centred                     three-centred

Ogee                            Segmental

Fig. 3    Arches

26

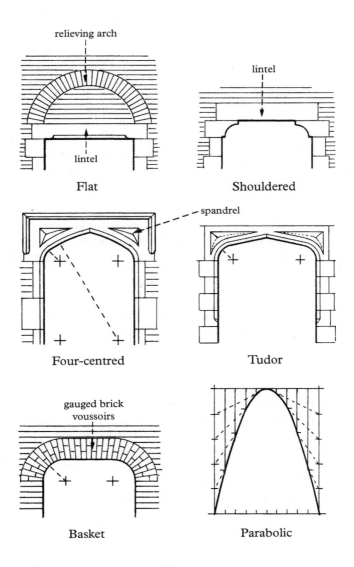

relieving arch

lintel

Flat

lintel

Shouldered

spandrel

Four-centred

Tudor

gauged brick voussoirs

Basket

Parabolic

**ARCH** [3] Types include: **BASKET ARCH** or **ANSE DE PANIER** (French, *lit.* basket handle): three-centred and *depressed*, or with a flat centre. **CHANCEL**: dividing *chancel* from *nave* or *crossing* in a church. **CROSSING**: spanning *piers* at a crossing in a church. **DEPRESSED** or **THREE-CENTRED**: with a rounded top, but curving inward more at the sides. **FOUR-CENTRED**: with four arcs, the lower two curving inward more than the upper, with a blunt central point; typical of late medieval English architecture. **JACK ARCH**: shallow segmental *vault springing* from beams, used for fireproof floors, bridge decks, etc. **OGEE** (adjective ogival): a pointed arch with a double reverse curve, especially popular in the 14th century; a *nodding ogee* curves forward from the wall face at the top. **PARABOLIC**: shaped like a chain suspended from two level points, but inverted. **RELIEVING** or **DISCHARGING**: incorporated in a wall to relieve superimposed weight. **SHOULDERED**: with arcs in each corner and a flat centre or *lintel*. **SKEW**: spanning *responds* not diametrically opposed. **STILTED**: with a vertical section above the *impost* i.e. the horizontal *moulding* at the springing. **STRAINER**: inserted in an opening to resist inward pressure. **THREE-CENTRED**: see Depressed, above. **TRANSVERSE**: spanning a main axis (e.g. of a vaulted space). **TRIUMPHAL ARCH**: influential type of Imperial *Roman* monument, free-standing, with a square *attic* or top section and broad sections to either side of the main opening, often with lesser openings or *columns*. **TUDOR**: with arcs in each corner joining straight lines to the central point. **TWO-CENTRED**: the simplest kind of pointed arch.

**ARCHAEOLOGICAL** In architecture, the accurate detailed use of a revived style, e.g. Greek or *Gothic*; hence archaeologically correct.

**ARCHED BRACES** Curved paired *braces* forming an *arch* in a timber roof, connecting wall or *post* below with *tie-beam* or *collar-beam* above [34].

**ARCHITRAVE** Formalized *lintel*, the lowest member of the *entablature* in *classical* architecture [23]. Also the moulded frame of a door or window (often borrowing the profile of a classical architrave). **LUGGED**: a moulded frame with horizontal projections at the top [20]. **SHOULDERED**: similar, but with vertical projections in addition [30].

**ARCHIVOLT**   Under-surface of an *arch*, or a moulded band following its contour.

**ARCUATED**   Dependent structurally on the *arch* principle. Compare *trabeated*.

**ARK**   Chest or cupboard housing the tables of Jewish law in a synagogue.

**ARRIS**   Sharp edge where two surfaces meet at an angle [23].

**ARROW LOOP**   A *loophole* (vertical slit window) in the walls of a castle, with *splayed* inner *jambs* to allow the firing of arrows.

**ART DECO**   A style of the 1920s and 30s, using bold simplified patterns and bright colours, often combining self-consciously up-to-date motifs with others derived from non-European or 'primitive' art. The name derives from the Exposition Internationale des Arts Décoratifs et Industriels Modernes, held in Paris in 1925. Its boundaries overlap with *Expressionism* and *Modernism* [pl. 33].

**ART NOUVEAU**   A European decorative style at its peak *c.* 1890–1910, marked by swirling ornament derived from natural forms. True Art Nouveau design aimed to be distinct from all previous styles. Compare *Free Style*.

**ARTISAN MANNERISM**   Describes the decorative *classical* architecture of mid-17th-century England, of which master masons and other craftsmen were the chief exponents; so called because of certain affinities with Continental Mannerism. It is looser and more eclectic than the *Palladian* style of the same period [pl. 14].

**ARTS AND CRAFTS**   Associated with the Arts and Crafts movement, an important offshoot of the later English *Gothic Revival*. Not so much a style as an approach to design, it sought truth to materials, high standards of craftsmanship, and an integration of decorative and fine arts, architecture included. Its representative figure is the writer and designer William Morris (1834–96) [pls 49, 51].

**ASHLAR**   Masonry of large blocks worked to even faces and square edges [29]. **BROACHED ASHLAR** (Scots): scored with parallel lines made by a narrow-pointed chisel (broach). **DROVED ASHLAR** (Scots): similar but with lines made by a broad chisel.

**ASHLAR PIECE**   In a timber roof, a short vertical piece connecting inner *wall-plate* or timber pad to rafter [34].

**ASTRAGAL**   *Classical moulding* of semicircular section [23]. Also (Scots) glazing bar between window panes.

**ASTYLAR**   Of a *classical* building: with no *columns* or vertical features.

**ATLANTES**   (*lit.* Atlas figures): Male figures supporting an *entablature*; their female counterparts are *caryatids*.

**ATRIUM** (plural: atria)   Open inner court of a house, especially a *Roman* house; in a *multi-storey* building, a toplit covered court rising through all storeys.

**ATTACHED COLUMN**   One that partly merges into a wall or *pier*.

**ATTIC**   Small top storey within a roof. Also the storey above the main *entablature* of a *classical* façade.

**ATTIC BASE**   In *classical* architecture, a type of *base* used on *columns* especially of the *Ionic* type, with two large convex rings joined by a spreading convex *moulding* [23].

**AUMBRY**   In a church or chapel, a recess or cupboard to hold sacred vessels for the Mass.

**BAG-RUBBED POINTING** *Pointing* (exposed mortar jointing) that is flush at the edges and gently recessed in the middle. To be distinguished from bucket-handle pointing, where the concavity is emphasized.

**BAILEY** An enclosure defended by a ditch and palisade, usually as part of a *motte-and-bailey* castle.

**BALANCE BEAM** (Canals): Beam projecting horizontally from the top of a lock gate, enabling it to be opened and closed manually.

**BALCONETTE** A small balcony or window-guard attached to an individual window.

**BALDACCHINO** Free-standing canopy, originally fabric, over an altar. Compare *ciborium*.

**BALLFLOWER** Globular flower of three petals enclosing a ball. Typical of the years *c.* 1300–30, during the *Decorated* phase of English medieval architecture [21].

**BALUSTER, BALUSTRADE** *Pillar* or *pedestal* of bellied form. **BALUSTERS**: vertical supports of this or any other form, for a handrail or *coping*, the whole being called a balustrade [32]. **BLIND BALUSTRADE**: the same applied to the wall surface. A **SPLAT BALUSTER** is flat and has shaped sides.

**BANDED RUSTICATION** *Rustication* (the exaggerated treatment of masonry to give an effect of strength), with only the horizontal joints emphasized.

**BAPTISTERY** Division of a church designed to house the *font*; also a separate building for the same purpose.

**BAR TRACERY** A form of *tracery* introduced *c.* 1250, in which patterns are formed by intersecting moulded ribwork continuing upwards from the *mullions*. It was especially elaborate during the *Decorated* period of English *Gothic*, i.e. *c.* 1290–*c.* 1400 [4].

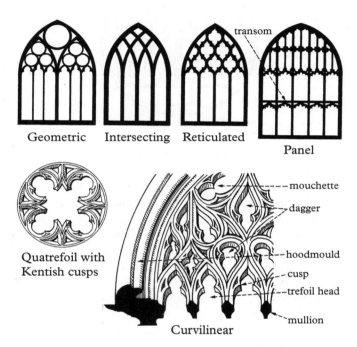

Geometric    Intersecting    Reticulated

Panel

Quatrefoil with Kentish cusps

mouchette

dagger

hoodmould

cusp

trefoil head

mullion

Curvilinear

Fig. 4   Bar tracery

**BARBICAN** Outwork defending the entrance to a castle.

**BARGEBOARDS** (corruption of 'vergeboards') Boards, often carved or pierced (called *fretted*), fixed beneath the *eaves* of a *gable* to cover and protect the *rafters*.

**BARLEY-SUGAR COLUMNS** *Columns* with twisted spiral *shafts*. Also called *Salomonic* or *Solomonic columns*, after columns in Rome supposed to have come from Solomon's Temple in Jerusalem.

**BARMKIN** (Scots): Wall enclosing courtyard attached to a *tower house*.

1. *Anglo-Saxon*: Colchester, Holy Trinity, w doorway. *Essex*

2. *Norman*: Edstaston, St Mary, s doorway of nave, late C12. *Shropshire*

3. *Norman*: Waltham Abbey, Holy Cross and St Lawrence, second quarter of the C12. *Essex*

4. *Transitional*: Worcester Cathedral, two w bays of nave, *c.* 1175–85.
*Worcestershire*

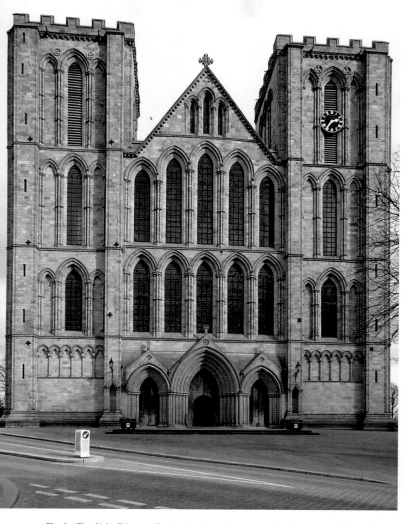

5. *Early English*: Ripon Cathedral, w front, probably 1230s. *Yorkshire West Riding: Leeds, Bradford and the North*

6. *Decorated (Geometric)*: Ripon Cathedral, E end, after 1284. *Yorkshire ls, Bradford and the North*

Pevsner's Architectural Glossary
ISBN 978-0-300-16721-4
*erratum*
colour illustrations 1 and 2, facing p. 32,
are transposed

7. *Decorated (Curvilinear)*: Chaddesley Corbett, St Cassian,
E window, mid-C14. *Worcestershire*

8. *Decorated*: Kidwelly, St Mary, Carmarthenshire, piscina and
sedilia, C14. *Carmarthenshire and Ceredigion*

9. Worcester Cathedral, misericord, jousting scene, *c.* 1397.
*Worcestershire*

10. *Perpendicular / Tudor*: Sefton, St Helen, parclose screen, early C16.
*Lancashire: Liverpool and the South-West*

11. *Decorated*: Pershore Abbey, chancel vault, probably *c.* 1290–1300. *Worcestershire*

12. *Perpendicular / Tudor*: Gestingthorpe, St Mary, double-hammer-beam roof attributed to Thomas Loveday, *c.* 1525. *Essex*

13. *Perpendicular / Tudor*: Westminster Abbey, Chapel of Henry VII, *c.* 1503–12, vault attributed to William Vertue. *London 6: Westminster*

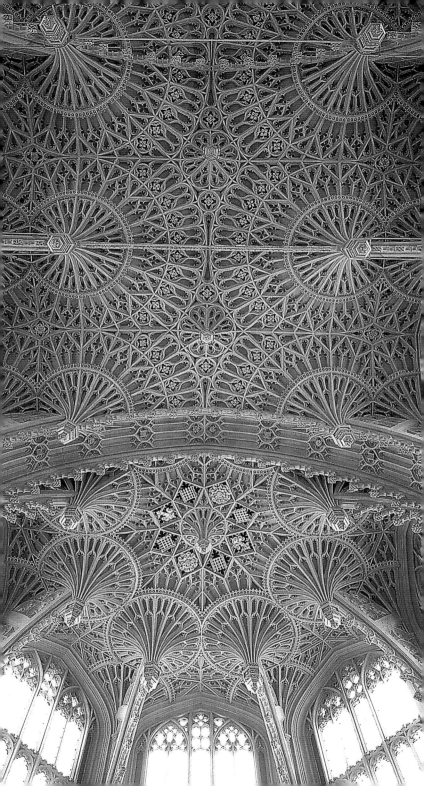

14. *Baroque / Artisan Mannerist*: Minsterley, Holy Trinity, by William Taylor, 1688–9, w front. *Shropshire*

15. *Baroque*: Christ Church, Spitalfields, 1714–29, by Nicholas Hawksmoor, w front. *London 5: East*

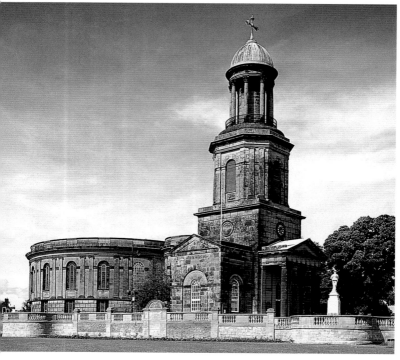

16. *Gothic Revival / Gothick*: Croome D'Abitot, St Mary Magdalene, 1759–63, almost certainly by Lancelot Brown. *Worcestershire*

17. *Neo-classical*: Shrewsbury, St Chad, by George Steuart, 1790–2. *Shropshire*

18. *Gothic Revival / Gothick*: Liverpool, St George, Heyworth Street, Everton, built by John Cragg, 1813–14. *Liverpool City Guide*

19. *Gothic Revival*: Alvechurch, St Laurence, 1857–61, by William Butterfield. *Worcestershire*

20. *Gothic Revival*: Brighton, St Michael and All Angels, nave by
William Burges, 1893–5. *Brighton and Hove City Guide*

21. *Neo-Byzantine*: Bradford, Heaton, Our Lady and the First
    Martyrs, by J.H. Langtry-Langton, 1935, interior. *Yorkshire
    West Riding: Leeds, Bradford and the North*

22. *Modernist*: London, St Paul, Bow Common, by Maguire &
    Murray, 1956–60, interior. *London 5: East*

**BAROQUE** The term, originally derogatory, for a style at its peak in 17th- and early 18th-century Europe, which developed the *classical* architecture of the *Renaissance* towards greater extravagance and drama. Its innovations included greater freedom from the conventions of the *orders*, much interplay of concave and convex forms, and a preference for the single visual sweep. The revival of the style in early 20th-century Britain, often termed Edwardian Baroque or *Neo-Baroque*, drew more on English prototypes than on the more expansive variants of the Continent [pls 14, 15, 27, 28].

**BARREL VAULT** The simplest kind of *vault*, in the form of a continuous semicircular or (less commonly) pointed *arch*; also called a *tunnel vault*.

**BARROW** Burial mound.

**BARTIZAN** *Corbelled* turret, square or round, frequently at an angle [35].

**BASCULE** Hinged part of a lifting (or bascule) bridge.

**BASE** Moulded foot of a *column* or *pilaster*. An *Attic base* is the form used on an *Ionic* column, with two large convex rings joined by a spreading convex *moulding*.

**BASE CRUCK** A type of timber construction in which curving paired members (*blades*) rise from ground level to a *tie-beam* or *collar-beam* which supports the roof timbers [11].

**BASEMENT** Lowest, subordinate storey; hence the lowest part of a *classical elevation*, below the *piano nobile* or principal storey.

**BASILICA** A *Roman* public hall; hence an *aisled* building, especially a church, with a *clerestory*, i.e. windows in the walls rising over the aisles.

**BASKET ARCH** An *arch* where the height is less than half the span. It may be three-centred, or with a flat middle section [3]; also called *anse de panier* (French, *lit.* basket handle).

**BASTION** One of a series of defensive semicircular or polygonal projections from the main wall of a fortress or city.

**BATTER** Intentional inward inclination of a wall face.

**BATTLEMENT** Defensive *parapet*, composed of *merlons* (solid) and crenels or crenelles (*embrasures* or openings) through which archers could shoot; sometimes called *crenellation*. Also used decoratively. Irish battlements have the up-and-down rhythm of merlons and crenels interrupted at the corners, which are built up in a series of high steps; typical of late medieval Irish architecture.

**BAWN** (Irish, *lit.* ox fold): Defensive walled enclosure attached to, or near, a *tower house* or Plantation castle. See *Barmkin* (Scots).

**BAY** Division of an *elevation* or interior space as defined by regular vertical features such as *arches*, *columns*, windows etc.

**BAY LEAF** *Classical* ornament of overlapping bay leaves [23].

**BAY WINDOW** Window of one or more storeys projecting from the face of a building. **CANTED**: with a straight front and angled sides. **BOW WINDOW**: curved. **ORIEL**: rests on *corbels* or *brackets* and starts above ground level; also the window in the bay at the upper or *dais* end of a medieval great hall.

**BEAD-AND-REEL** A type of *classical* ornament resembling a string of convex- and concave-ended beads [23].

**BEAKHEAD** *Norman* enrichment with a row of beaked bird or beast heads usually biting into a *roll moulding* [21].

**BEAUX-ARTS** An approach to *classical* design associated with the École des Beaux Arts in Paris, at the peak of its influence in the later 19th and early 20th centuries. It is marked by strong axial planning and the grandiose but rigorous use of the *orders*.

**BEE-BOLL** (Scots): Wall recess to contain a beehive.

**BELFAST ROOF TRUSS** A wide segmental *truss* (a rigid frame spanning a space or opening) built as a lattice-beam, originally using short cuts of timber left over from shipbuilding in Belfast.

**BELFRY** Chamber or stage in a tower where bells are hung.

**BELL CAPITAL** A form of *capital* shaped like an upturned bell, common in early medieval architecture [5].

**BELLCAST ROOF** (Scots): A sloping roof swept out slightly over the *eaves*. In England often called a *sprocketed* roof.

**BELLCOTE** Small *gabled* or roofed housing for a bell or bells.

**BERM** Level area separating a ditch from a bank on a *hill-fort* or *barrow*.

Fig. 5   Bell capital

**BILLET**   *Norman* ornament of small half-cylindrical or rectangular blocks [21].

**BIVALLATE**   Of a *hill-fort*: defended by two concentric banks and ditches.

**BLADE**   In timber construction, one of the paired inclined timbers making up a *cruck* [11].

**BLIND ARCADE**   A series of *arches* supported by *piers* or *columns*, applied to the wall surface.

**BLIND BALUSTRADE**   A *balustrade* (a row of balusters) applied to the wall surface.

**BLIND PORTICO**   The front features of a *portico* applied to a wall.

**BLIND TRACERY**   *Tracery* applied to a solid wall.

**BLOCK CAPITAL**   A *capital* shaped like a cube with rounded convex lower parts, common in *Norman* architecture [21].

**BLOCKED**   Interrupted by regular projecting blocks (blocking), as on a *Gibbs surround* [15].

**BLOCKING COURSE**   *Course* of stones, or equivalent, on top of a *cornice* and crowning the wall.

**BOARD-MARKED**   Of *concrete*, with the impression of boards left by the temporary *timber framing* (*formwork*) used for casting.

**BOISERIES**   (French): *Panelling* or other fitted interior woodwork with elaborate decoration of foliage, etc., used especially in the 17th- to 19th-century France.

**BOLECTION MOULDING**   A convex *moulding* covering the joint between two different planes, especially on *panelling* and fireplace surrounds of the late 17th and early 18th centuries [24].

35

**BOND** The pattern of long sides (*stretchers*) and short ends (*headers*) produced by laying bricks in a particular way [6]. **ENGLISH BOND**: with alternate *courses* of headers and stretchers exposed. **ENGLISH GARDEN WALL BOND**: with one course of headers for every three or more courses of stretchers. **FLEMISH BOND**: with alternating stretchers and headers showing. **HEADER BOND**: with only the headers exposed. **STACK BOND**: non-structural brick facing in vertical (i.e. non-overlapping) tiers. **STRETCHER BOND**: with only the stretchers showing.

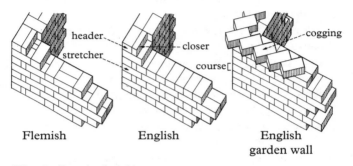

Flemish          English          English
                                  garden wall

Fig. 6   Bonds (brick)

**BOSS** Knob or projection, e.g. at the intersection of ribs in a *rib-vault* [37].

**BOW WINDOW** A projecting window of curved plan.

**BOWED GIRDER** A large beam with its top rising in an *arch*.

**BOWSTRING BRIDGE** A bridge with *arches* rising above the roadway which is suspended from them.

**BOWTELL** A term in use by the 15th century for a form of *roll moulding*, usually three-quarters of a circle in section (also called an *edge roll*).

**BOX FRAME** Timber-framed construction in which vertical and horizontal members support the roof [34]. Also *concrete* construction in which the loads are taken on cross-walls; also called *cross-wall construction*.

**BOX GIRDER** A large beam of hollow-box section.

**BOX PEW** *Pew* enclosed by a high wooden back and ends, the latter having doors.

**BRACE**  Subsidiary member of a structural frame or roof. Bracing is often arranged in decorative patterns in timber-framed buildings [34]. **ARCHED BRACES**: curved paired braces forming an *arch*, connecting wall or *post* below with *tie-beam* or *collar-beam* above. **PASSING BRACES**: long straight braces passing across other members of the *truss*. **SCISSOR BRACES**: paired braces crossing diagonally between pairs of *rafters* or *principals*. **WIND-BRACES**: short, usually curved braces connecting *side purlins* or *ridge-piece* with principals.

**BRACKET**  Small supporting piece of stone, etc., to carry a projecting horizontal member; hence also bracket-cornice.

**BRATTISHING**  Ornamental crest, often formed of leaves, flowers or miniature *battlements*, common in late medieval English architecture.

**BREASTSHOT WATER WHEEL**  One with water fed on to the wheel at mid-height, falling and passing beneath. Compare *overshot*, *pitchback* and *undershot*.

**BRESSUMER**  (*lit.* breast-beam): Big horizontal beam supporting the wall above, especially a *jetty* or projecting storey [34].

**BRETASCHE**  (*lit. battlement*): Defensive wooden *gallery* on a wall.

**BRISE-SOLEIL**  (French, *lit.* sun break): A screen of projecting fins or slats which deflect direct sunlight from windows.

**BROACH SPIRE**  A *spire* starting from a square *base*, then carried into an octagonal section by means of triangular faces [7].

**BROCH**  (Scots): Circular tower-like structure, open in the middle, the double wall of *dry-stone* masonry linked by slabs forming internal galleries at varying levels; found in west and north Scotland and mostly dating from between 100 B.C. and A.D. 100.

**BROKEN PEDIMENT**  A *pediment* with its apex omitted [25].

**BRONZE AGE**  The period from *c.* 2000 B.C. to 800-600 B.C., characterized by the use of bronze or copper tools or weapons.

**BRUTALISM**  A tendency within Modernist architecture of the later 1950s to 1970s marked by the display of rough

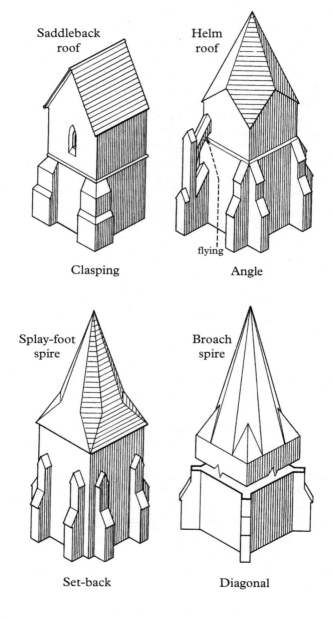

Saddleback
roof

Helm
roof

Clasping

Angle

flying

Splay-foot
spire

Broach
spire

Set-back

Diagonal

Fig. 7  Buttresses, roofs and spires

38

or unfinished *concrete*, large massive forms, and abrupt juxtapositions.

**BUCRANIUM** (plural: bucrania)   Ox skull used decoratively in *friezes* on *classical* buildings, especially those of the *Doric order.*

**BULL-NOSED SILL**   *Sill* displaying a pronounced convex upper edge.

**BULLSEYE WINDOW**   Small oval window, set horizontally. Also called an *oeil de boeuf.*

**BUSH-HAMMERED**   Of *concrete*, textured with steel bushes or brushes after casting; also called brushed.

**BUT-AND-BEN**   (Scots, *lit.* outer and inner rooms): Two-room cottage.

**BUTT PURLINS**   *Purlins* (horizontal longitudinal timbers in a roof structure) tenoned into either side of the *principals* [34]. Also called *tenoned purlins.*

**BUTTERY**   In a medieval house or college, a store room off the *screens passage*, especially for drink; compare *pantry.*

**BUTT-JOINT**   A joint in which the stones or bricks do not overlap.

**BUTTRESS**   Vertical member projecting from a wall to stabilize it or to resist the lateral thrust of an *arch*, roof or *vault* [7, 37]. **ANGLE BUTTRESS**: set at 90 degrees at the angle of a building. **CLASPING BUTTRESS**: one which encases the angle. **DIAGONAL BUTTRESS**: set diagonally to the angle. A **FLYING BUTTRESS** transmits the thrust to a heavy *abutment* by means of an arch or half-arch. A **SET-BACK BUTTRESS** is placed slightly back from the angle.

**BYZANTINE**   A style which originated at Byzantium (Constantinople), the Eastern capital of the Roman Empire, in the 5th century, spreading around the Mediterranean and, with Eastern (Orthodox) Christianity, from Sicily to Russia in later centuries. It developed the round *arches*, *vaults* and domes of *Roman* architecture but eschewed formalized *classical* detail in favour of lavish decoration and ornament of emblematic and symbolic significance. Introduced to late 19th- and early 20th-century Britain as an alternative to *Gothic*, usually for church architecture; often called *Neo-Byzantine.*

**CABLE MOULDING**   A *moulding* like twisted strands of a rope; also called *rope moulding*.

**CADAVER**   In a monument, an effigy depicted a naked corpse; also called a *gisant*.

**CAMBER**   Slight rise or upward curve in place of a horizontal line or plane.

**CAMES**   Lead strips joining pieces of window glass.

**CAMPANILE**   (Italian): Free-standing bell-tower.

**CANDLE-SNUFFER ROOF**   Conical roof of a turret [35].

**CANTED**   With an angled edge or sides.

**CANTILEVER**   Horizontal projection (e.g. step, canopy) supported at one end only.

**CAPHOUSE**   (Scots): Small chamber at the head of a turnpike or *newel* stair, opening onto the *parapet* walk. Also a chamber rising from within the parapet walk [35].

**CAPITAL**   Head or crowning feature of a *column* or *pilaster* [5, 10, 23, 33, 36, 40].

**CARREL**   Compartment designed for individual work or study.

**CARTOUCHE**   *Classical* tablet with ornate frame [25].

**CARYATIDS**   Female figures supporting an *entablature*; their male counterparts are *Atlantes*.

**CASEMATE**   *Vaulted* chamber, with *embrasures* (*splayed* openings) for defence, within a castle wall or projecting from it.

**CASEMENT**   Side-hinged window.

**CAST IRON**   Hard and brittle iron, cast in a mould to the required shape rather than forged. Compare *wrought iron*.

**CASTELLATED**   With *battlements*.

**CATSLIDE**   A roof continuing down in one plane over a lower projection [14].

**CAVETTO**   *Classical* concave *moulding* of quarter-round section [23].

**CELL**   One of a series of small rooms; also a compartment of a *groin-vault* or *rib-vault*.

**CELLA**   The main body or enclosure of a *classical* temple, as distinct from the *portico*. Also called a *naos*.

**CELLURACH**   (Irish, *lit.* a *cell* or church): A walled enclosure, often near old monastic sites, used until recent times for the burial of unbaptized children. Also called a *killeen*.

**CELURE OR CEILURE**   Enriched area of roof above a *rood* or altar.

**CEMENT**   Calcined lime or clay. From the mid-19th century, often used to mean the Portland Cement patented in 1824 by Joseph Aspdin. Because it sets harder and faster than lime mortar, it is popular with builders, who know it as 'OPC'. **CEMENT RENDERING**: a cheaper substitute for *stucco* (fine lime plaster), usually with a grainy texture.

**CENOTAPH**   (*lit.* empty tomb): Funerary monument which is not a burying place.

**CENTRING**   Wooden support for the building of an *arch* or *vault*, removed after completion.

**CHAMBERED TOMB**   *Neolithic* burial mound with a stone-built chamber and entrance passage covered by an earthen *barrow* or stone cairn.

**CHAMFER**   (*lit.* corner-break): Surface formed by cutting off a square edge or corner [8]. **DOUBLE CHAMFER**: applied to each of two recessed *arches* [13]. **HOLLOW CHAMFER**: with a concave surface. **SUNK CHAMFER**: recessed more deeply into the surface.

**CHAMFERSTOP**   The junction between a *chamfer* (surface formed by cutting off a square edge or corner) and a straight edge [8].

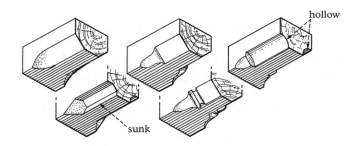

Fig. 8   Chamfers and chamferstops

**CHANCEL**   The eastern part or end of a church, where the altar is placed; usually set apart for the clergy.

**CHANCEL ARCH**   In a church, an *arch* dividing *chancel* from *nave* or *crossing*.

**CHANNELLED RUSTICATION**   *Rustication* (the exaggerated treatment of masonry to give an effect of strength), with the horizontal and vertical joints emphasized [29].

**CHANTRY CHAPEL**   A chapel, often attached to or within a church, endowed for the celebration of masses principally for the soul of the founder(s).

**CHAPTER HOUSE**   The place of assembly for the members of a monastery or cathedral, usually located off the east side of the *cloister*.

**CHECK**   (Scots): A rectangular section cut out of a masonry edge to receive a shutter, door, window etc.; also called a *rebate*.

**CHEQUER-SET**   Of *corbelling*, with corbels set touching at different depths [35].

**CHEQUERWORK**   A pattern of chequered squares made with contrasting materials.

**CHERRY-CAULKING OR CHERRY-COCKING**   (Scots): Decorative masonry technique using lines of tiny stones (*pins or pinning*) in the mortar joints. In England, known as *galleting*.

**CHEVET**   (*lit.* head): French term for a *chancel* with a surrounding *aisle* (called an *ambulatory*) and *radiating chapels*.

**CHEVRON** V-shape used in series or (later) double series on a *moulding* in *Norman* architecture [21]. Also (especially when on a single plane) called *zigzag*.

**CHINOISERIE** (French): The European imitation of Chinese motifs in the mid-18th century, seen most commonly in the decorative arts, but also used for interiors and for the occasional complete building.

**CHIP-CARVING** Simple geometrical patterns cut into a surface.

**CHOIR** The part of a cathedral, monastic church or *collegiate church* where services are sung.

**CHURCHWARDEN'S PEW** An especially tall or elaborate *pew* for use by the churchwarden, usually placed at the west end of a church.

**CIBORIUM** A fixed canopy over an altar, usually *vaulted* and supported on four *columns*; also called a *baldacchino*. Also a canopied shrine for the reserved sacrament.

**CINQUECENTO** (Italian): The Italian *Renaissance* architecture of the 16th century; also used for its 19th-century revival.

**CINQUEFOIL** A five-lobed opening.

**CIST** Stone-lined or slab-built grave.

**CLACHAN** (Scots): A hamlet or small village; also, a village inn.

**CLADDING** External covering or skin applied to a structure, especially a *framed building*.

**CLAPBOARDING** The North American term for *weatherboarding*, i.e. wall *cladding* of overlapping horizontal boards.

**CLAPPER BRIDGE** A bridge with single flat stone slabs forming the roadway.

**CLASP** (Consortium Local Authorities Special Programme): A kind of *system building* using light steel framing, suitable for schools etc., employed in the United Kingdom from the 1950s.

**CLASPED PURLINS** In a timber roof, *purlins* or horizontal longitudinal timbers which rest on *queenposts* or are carried in the angle between *principals* and *collar* [34].

**CLASPING BUTTRESS** A *buttress* which encases the angle [7].

**CLASSICAL**   A term used for the architecture of Ancient Greece and Rome, revived at the *Renaissance* and subsequently imitated around the Western world. It uses a range of conventional forms, the roots of which are the *orders*, or types of *column* each with its fixed proportions and ornaments (especially *Doric, Ionic* and *Corinthian*). Classical buildings tend also to be symmetrical, both externally and on plan. Classical architecture in England began *c.* 1530 with applied ornamental motifs, followed within a few decades by fully-fledged new buildings [pls 30, 31].

**CLERESTORY OR CLEARSTOREY**   Uppermost storey of a church, pierced by windows. Also high-level windows in secular buildings.

**CLOISTER**   An enclosed quadrangle in a monastery or by a church, surrounded by covered passages; by extension, any space so enclosed. **CLOISTER GARTH**: the area enclosed by a cloister.

**CLOSE**   The precinct of a cathedral. Also (Scots) a courtyard or passage giving access to a number of buildings.

**CLOSE STUDDING**   Of a timber-framed wall: with closely set *studs* or vertical timbers of equal size [34].

**CLOSED STRING**   A sloping member of a staircase covering the ends of the *treads* and *risers*, with a continuous upper edge [32]; hence a closed string staircase. Compare *open string*.

**CLOSED TRUSS**   Of a roof: with the spaces between the timbers filled, to form an internal partition or partitions.

**CLOSER**   A brick cut to complete a *bond* [6].

**CLUSTER BLOCK**   *Multi-storey* flats with the individual flats arranged around a service core.

**COADE STONE**   Ceramic artificial stone made 1769– *c.* 1840 in Lambeth, South London by Eleanor Coade (d. 1821) and her associates.

**COB**   Walling material of clay mixed with straw. Also called *pisé* and, in Cumberland, clay dabbin.

**COFFERING**   Arrangement of sunken panels (coffers), square or polygonal, decorating a ceiling, *vault* or *arch*.

**COGGING**   A decorative *course* of bricks laid diagonally [6].

**COLLAR OR COLLAR-BEAM** Horizontal transverse roof-timber connecting a pair of *rafters* or *cruck blades*, set between the apex and the *wall-plate* [34].

**COLLAR PURLIN** Central roof-timber which carries *collar-beams* and is supported by *crown-posts*. Also called a *crown-plate*.

**COLLEGIATE** (of church seating): Arranged in confronted rows facing north and south, rather than towards the altar; so called after the chapels of the older university colleges.

**COLLEGIATE CHURCH** A church endowed for the support of a college of priests.

**COLONNADE** Range of *columns* supporting an *entablature*, without *arches*. Compare *arcade*.

**COLONNETTE** A small *column* or *shaft*, usually medieval.

**COLOSSAL ORDER** In *classical* architecture, an *order* whose height is that of two or more storeys of the building to which it is applied. Also called a *giant order*.

**COLUMBARIUM** Shelved, niched structure to house multiple burials.

**COLUMN** An upright structural member, especially in the *classical* styles, of round section and with a *shaft*, a *capital*, and usually a *base* [23, 27].

**COLUMN FIGURE** Carved figure attached to a medieval *column* or *shaft*, usually flanking a doorway. Compare *trumeau figure*.

**COLUMNA ROSTRATA** (Latin): *Column* decorated with carved prows of ships to celebrate a naval victory.

**COMMISSIONERS' CHURCH** An Anglican church built with public money by the Church Building Commissioners, in the period 1818–56.

**COMMISSIONERS' GOTHIC** A reference to the Commission established by Parliament to provide new churches in areas where late 18th-century and early 19th-century industrialization was provoking rapid urbanization. The kind of *Gothic Revival* style used for many of the *Commissioners' churches* after 1818. It tends to be more accurate in terms of archaeology than the so-called *Gothick* of the 18th century, but is often let down by cheapness or thinness of execution.

45

**COMMON BRICKS**  (often just 'commons'): See *place bricks*.

**COMMON RAFTERS**  Regularly spaced uniform *rafters* placed along the length of the roof, or between *principals* [34]; also called *coupled rafters*. A common rafter or coupled rafter roof has pairs of rafters only, i.e. without principal and lesser rafters used in combination.

**COMMUNION RAILS**  In a church or chapel, *rails* used to enclose an area around the altar or *communion table*.

**COMMUNION TABLE**  Table used in Protestant churches for the celebration of Holy Communion.

**COMPOSITE**  One of the *orders* of *classical* architecture in which the *capital* of the *column* combines the *volutes* of the *Ionic order* with the foliage of the *Corinthian*.

**COMPOUND PIER**  A *pier* composed of grouped *shafts*, or a solid core surrounded by shafts.

**CONCRETE**  Composition of *cement* (calcined lime and clay), *aggregate* (small stones and rock chippings), sand and water. It can be poured into *formwork* or *shuttering* (temporary framing of timber or metal) on site (*in situ* concrete) or *pre-cast* as components before construction. **REINFORCED**: incorporating steel rods to take tensile forces. **PRE-STRESSED**: with tensioned steel rods. Finishes include the impression of boards left by formwork (*board-marked* or shuttered), and texturing with steel brushes (brushed or *bush-hammered*), picks or hammers (pick-hammered or *hammer-dressed*).

**CONDUCTOR**  (Scots): Down-pipe for rainwater.

**CONDUIT**  A water pipe; by extension, a public water-source, often architecturally or decoratively treated.

**CONSOLE**  *Bracket* of curved outline [9, 25].

Fig. 9   Console

**COOMB OR COMB CEILING**   (Scots): With sloping sides corresponding to the roof pitch up to a flat centre.

**COPING**   Protective *course* of masonry or brickwork capping a wall [29].

**CORBEL**   Projecting block supporting something above [34]. **CORBEL COURSE**: continuous *course* of projecting stones or bricks fulfilling the same function. **CORBEL TABLE**: series of corbels to carry a *parapet* or a *wall-plate* or *wall-post*. **CORBELLING**: brick or masonry courses built out beyond one another to support a chimneystack, window, etc. [35]; variants include continuous corbelling, i.e. of one even profile, and *chequer-set* corbelling, with corbels set touching and at different depths.

**CORBIESTEPS**   (Scots): Squared stones set like steps, e.g. on a *gable*. Also called *crowsteps*.

**CORINTHIAN**   The most slender and ornate of the three main *classical orders*. It has a basket-shaped *capital* ornamented with *acanthus* foliage [23].

**CORNICE**   Flat-topped ledge with moulded underside, projecting along the top of a building or feature, especially as the highest member of the *classical entablature* [23]. Also the decorative *moulding* in the angle between wall and ceiling. An **EAVES CORNICE** overhangs the edge of a roof.

**CORPS-DE-LOGIS**   (French): The main building(s) as distinct from the wings or *pavilions*.

**COSMATI WORK**   A form of mosaic using simple geometrical patterns and coloured stones, developed in Italy in the 12th and 13th centuries.

**COTTAGE ORNÉ**   (French): An artfully rustic small house associated with the *Picturesque* movement.

**COUNTERCHANGING**   Of *joists* on a ceiling divided by beams into compartments, when placed in opposite directions in alternate squares.

**COUNTERSCARP BANK**   Low bank on the downhill or outer side of a hillfort ditch.

**COUPLED RAFTERS**   Regularly spaced uniform *rafters* (inclined lateral timbers supporting the roof covering) placed along the length of a roof or between principal rafters; also called *common rafters*.

**COUR D'HONNEUR**  (French): Formal entrance court before a house, usually with flanking wings and a screen wall or gates.

**COURSE**  Continuous layer of stones, bricks etc. in a wall [6].

**COVE**  A broad concave *moulding*, e.g. to mask the *eaves* of a roof. **COVED CEILING**: with a pronounced cove joining the walls to a flat central panel smaller than the whole area of the ceiling.

**CRADLE ROOF**  A timber roof with close-set *braces* of polygonal or curved profile, often ceiled between the timbers; also called a *wagon roof*.

**CREDENCE**  In churches, a shelf within or beside a *piscina*, or a table for the sacramental elements and vessels.

**CRENELLATION**  A defensive feature on a *parapet*, so called from the crenels or regular openings in it [35]; the whole forming *battlements*.

**CRINKLE–CRANKLE WALL**  Garden wall undulating in a series of serpentine curves, especially in Suffolk.

**CROCKETS**  In *Gothic* architecture, leafy hooks or knobs, as on a crocket *capital* [10]. Crocketing (rows of crockets) decorates the edges of *pinnacles*, canopies, etc.

Fig. 10   Crocket capital

**CROSSING**  In a church, the central space at the junction of the *nave*, *chancel* and *transepts*. **CROSSING ARCH**: an *arch* spanning *piers* at a crossing. **CROSSING TOWER**: a tower above a crossing.

**CROSS-WALL CONSTRUCTION**  Framed construction in which the loads are taken by cross-walls of *concrete* or brick. The external lateral walls are not usually load-bearing. In domestic buildings, almost exclusive to terrace housing built by public authorities in the 1960s and 70s.

**CROSS-WINDOW** A window with one *mullion* one *transom*, forming a cross-shape.

**CROWN** The upper part of an *arch* or *vault*.

**CROWN-PLATE** Central roof-timber which carries *collar-beams* and is supported by *crown-posts* [34]. Also called a *collar purlin*.

**CROWN-POST** A vertical timber in a roof structure, set centrally on a *tie-beam* and supporting a *collar purlin*, with longitudinal *braces* to it [34]. In an open *truss*, additional braces may rise laterally to the *collar-beam*; in a *closed truss* they may descend to the tie-beam.

**CROWSTEPS** Squared stones set like steps, e.g. on a *gable* [14, 35]. In Scotland also called *corbiesteps*.

**CRUCKS** (*lit.* crooked): Pairs of inclined timbers (*blades*), usually curved, set at *bay*-length intervals in a building; they support the roof timbers and, in timber buildings, also support the walls [11]. **BASE CRUCKS** have blades rising from ground level to a *tie-beam* or *collar-beam* which supports the roof timbers. **FULL CRUCKS** have blades rising from ground level to the apex of the roof, serving as the main members of a roof *truss*. **JOINTED CRUCKS** have blades formed from more than one timber; the lower member may act as a *wall-post*; it is usually elbowed at *wall-plate* level and jointed just above. **MIDDLE CRUCKS** have blades rising from halfway up the walls to a tie or collar-beam. **RAISED CRUCKS** have blades rising from halfway up the walls to the apex. **UPPER CRUCKS** have blades supported on a tie-beam and rising to the apex.

**CRYPT** Underground or half-underground area, usually below the east end of a church. **RING CRYPT**: corridor crypt surrounding the *apse* of an early medieval church, often associated with chambers for relics.

**CUPOLA** (*lit.* dome): Especially, a small dome on a circular or polygonal *base* crowning a larger dome, roof, or turret. Also (Scots) a small dome or skylight as an internal feature, especially over a stairwell.

**CURSUS** A long avenue defined by two parallel earthen banks with ditches outside.

**CURTAIN WALL** A non-load-bearing external wall applied to a framed structure, in architecture of the 20th century onwards. Also a connecting wall between the towers of a castle.

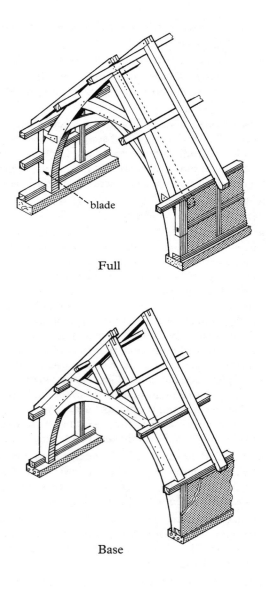

Full

blade

Base

Fig. 11   Cruck frames

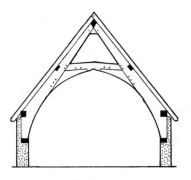

Raised

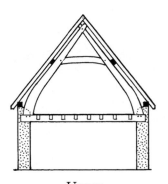

Upper

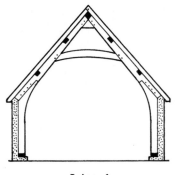

Jointed

**CURVILINEAR TRACERY**   *Bar tracery* with uninterrupted flowing curves, typical of the 14th century [4; pl. 7]; also called *flowing tracery*.

**CUSPS**   Projecting points formed by curves within the *arches* or *tracery* of *Gothic* architecture [4]. A *Kentish cusp* or *split cusp* has a v-shaped opening set within the apex. In *sub-cusping* the sides of the cusps have smaller cusps, usually on a recessed plane.

**CUTWATER**   A curved- or angle-ended stage at the bottom of a bridge *pier*.

**CYCLOPEAN MASONRY**   Large irregular polygonal stones, smooth and finely jointed.

**CYMA RECTA AND CYMA REVERSA**   *Classical mouldings* with double curves [23].

**DADO** The finishing (often with *panelling*) of the lower part of a wall, usually in a *classical* interior; in origin a formalized continuous *pedestal*. **DADO RAIL**: the *moulding* along the top of the dado.

**DAGGER** In *tracery*, an elongated *ogee*-ended lozenge shape [4].

**DAIS** A raised platform at one end of a medieval hall, where the lord or head of the household dined; also found in college or school halls, etc.

**DALLE-DE-VERRE** (French, *lit.* glass slab): A stained-glass technique invented in the mid-20th century, setting large, thick pieces of cast glass into a frame of *reinforced concrete* or epoxy resin.

**DECORATED** A distinctive phase of English *Gothic* which developed at the end of the 13th century and continued into the later 14th; sometimes abbreviated to Dec. Named from its elaborate window *tracery*, which abandoned the simple circular forms of *Geometric* in favour of more varied patterns based on segments of circles. Dec tracery makes much use of *ogee* or reversed curves, which were combined in the 14th century to produce *reticulated* and *flowing tracery* composed of *trefoils*, *quatrefoils* and *dagger* shapes. Similar inventiveness is seen in the patterns produced by the lierne and *tierceron vaults* of the period, in the three-dimensional handling of wall surfaces broken up by canopy work and sculpture and in imaginative spatial planning making use of diagonal axes [pls 6, 8, 9, 11, 37].

**DEMI-OR HALF-COLUMN**  An *engaged column* half of whose circumference projects from the wall.

**DENTIL**  Small square block used in series in *classical cornices*. Dentilation is produced by the projection of alternating *headers*, i.e. the short faces of bricks, along cornices or *string courses* [23].

**DEPRESSED ARCH**  An *arch* with a rounded top, but curving inward more at the sides [3]; also called a *three-centred arch*.

**DIAGONAL BUTTRESS**  A *buttress* set diagonally to the angle [7].

**DIAGONAL RIB**  One of the main elements of a *rib-vault*, crossing diagonally and marking the main divisions (called *cells*) [37].

**DIAMOND-FACED RUSTICATION**  *Rustication* (the exaggerated treatment of masonry to give an effect of strength), with the faces treated like shallow pyramids [29].

**DIAPER**  Repetitive surface decoration of lozenges or squares flat or in relief. Achieved in brickwork with bricks of two colours.

**DIE**  The upright part of a *pedestal*, i.e. between *base* and *cornice*.

**DIOCLETIAN WINDOW**  A semicircular window with two *mullions*, as used in the Baths of Diocletian, Rome [12]. Also called a *thermal window*.

Fig. 12   Diocletian window

**DISCHARGING ARCH**  An *arch* incorporated in a wall to relieve superimposed weight. Also called a *relieving arch*.

**DISTYLE**  Of a porch or *portico*: having two *columns* [27].

**DOG-LEG STAIR**  With parallel flights rising alternately in opposite directions, without an open well [32].

**DOGTOOTH**  Ornament in the *Early English* period of *Gothic*, consisting of a series of small pyramids formed by four stylized canine teeth meeting at a point [21].

**DOOCOT**  (Scots): Dovecote. A lectern type is free-standing with a single-pitch roof, a beehive type is circular and diminishes towards the top.

**DORIC**  The simplest and plainest of the three main *classical orders*, featuring a *frieze* with *triglyphs* and *metopes*. A *Roman Doric column* has a simple round *capital* with a narrow neck band and a plain or fluted *shaft* [23]. A *Greek Doric* column has a thin spreading convex capital and no *base* to the column [23]. See *Tuscan.*

**DORMER**  Window projecting from the slope of a roof [14].

**DORMER HEAD**  *Gable* above a *dormer* (window projecting from the slope of a roof), often formed as a *pediment* [35].

**DORTER**  The dormitory of an abbey or monastery, traditionally placed in the east range off the *cloister*.

**DOSSERET**  An isolated section of *entablature* above a *column* or *pilaster*.

**DOUBLE CHAMFER**  A *chamfer* (surface formed by cutting off a square edge) applied to each of two recessed *arches* [13].

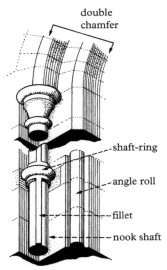

Fig. 13  Double chamfer

**DOUBLE PILE**  A row of rooms two deep.

**DOUBLE-FRAMED**  Of a roof: with longitudinal members such as *purlins* above the *springing* of the *rafters*. Compare *single-framed*.

**DRAGON BEAM**  In a timber-framed building, a horizontal beam set diagonally at the corner to carry the *joists* where two jetties or projecting storeys meet.

**DRESSINGS**  The stone or brickwork worked to a finished face about an angle, opening, or other feature.

**DRIPSTONE**  Moulded stone projecting from a wall to protect the lower parts from water; when over an opening, called a *hoodmould*.

**DRUM**  Circular or polygonal stage supporting a dome or *cupola*. Also one of the stones forming the *shaft* of a *column* [23].

**DRY-STONE**  Stone construction without mortar.

**DUN**  (Scots): Small stone-walled fort.

**DUTCH GABLE**  A *gable* with curved sides crowned by a *pediment* [14]. Also called a *Flemish gable*.

**EARED**  Of an *architrave* (a formalized *lintel*), with side projections at the top. Also called a *lugged* architrave [20].

**EARLY CHRISTIAN**  The style of the first Christian churches of the 4th and 5th centuries. As revived in 20th-century churches, it favours simplified *arcades* and round-arched openings, plain surfaces and tiled roofs.

**EARLY ENGLISH**  (E.E.): The first phase of English *Gothic* architecture, predominant in the period *c.* 1180–*c.* 1250, and making use of the pointed *arch* for openings and *vaulting*. Sometimes called *lancet* style from its use of single narrow windows. These can be grouped together under a common head of *plate tracery*. Larger arches frequently have narrow multiple *mouldings*, heavily undercut. *Stiff-leaf* ornament in high relief, and *compound piers* (i.e. with groups of *shafts*), often making use of *Purbeck* or, in the North of England, Frosterley marble, are also characteristic of the period [pl. 5].

**EASTER SEPULCHRE**  *Tomb-chest* used for Easter ceremonial, within or against the north wall of a *chancel* of a church or chapel.

**EAVES**  Overhanging edge of a roof; hence eaves *cornice* in this position.

**ECHINUS**  On a *Greek Doric column*, an *ovolo* or wide convex *moulding* below the *abacus* or top part of the *capital* [23].

**EDGE RAIL**  On a railway, a *rail* on which flanged wheels can run. Compare *plate rail*.

57

**EDGE ROLL**  A form of *roll moulding*, usually three-quarters of a circle in section (also called *bowtell*).

**EGG-AND-DART**  A type of *classical* ornament used on convex (*ovolo*) *mouldings*, based on alternate eggs and arrowheads [23].

**ELEVATION**  Any face of a building or side of a room. In a drawing, the same or any part of it, represented in two dimensions.

**ELIDED**  Used to describe a compound feature, e.g. an *entablature*, with some elements omitted or combined.

**ELIZABETHAN**  The English architecture of the later 16th century, marked by a decorative use of *Renaissance* ornament and a preference for symmetrical façades, usually with *gables* [pl. 40]. See also *Jacobean*.

**EMBATTLED**  With *battlements*.

**EMBRASURE**  *Splayed* opening in a wall or *battlement*.

**EN DÉLIT**  (French; *lit.* in error): Stone laid against the bed.

**ENCAUSTIC TILES**  Earthenware tiles fired with a pattern and glaze.

**ENFILADE**  Rooms in a formal series, usually with all the doorways on axis.

**ENGAGED COLUMN**  One that partly merges into a wall or *pier*. Also called an *attached column*.

**ENGINEERING BRICKS**  Dense bricks, originally used mostly for railway viaducts, etc, where they must withstand strong compressive forces.

**ENGLISH ALTAR**  The medieval type of altar with taller framed hangings on three sides, as revived in the late 19th century.

**ENGLISH BOND**  Brickwork with alternate *courses* of *headers* (short ends) and *stretchers* (long sides) exposed [6].

**ENGLISH GARDEN WALL BOND**  Brickwork with one *course* of *headers* (short ends) for every three or more courses of *stretchers* (long sides) [6].

**ENRICHMENTS**  The carved decoration of certain *classical mouldings* [23].

**ENTABLATURE**  In *classical* architecture, collective name for the three horizontal members (*architrave*, *frieze* and *cornice*) carried by a wall [23].

**ENTASIS**  Very slight convex deviation from a straight line, used to counter an optical illusion of concavity. Sometimes exaggerated into a deliberate parody of the *classical* rules, especially in early 20th-century buildings of the *Queen Anne* style.

**ENTRESOL**  *Mezzanine* floor subdividing what is structurally a single storey, e.g. a *vault*.

**EPITAPH**  Inscription on a tomb or monument.

**ESCUTCHEON**  Shield for a coat of arms or other heraldic display.

**EXEDRA**  In *classical* architecture, a large semicircular or polygonal recess; also called an *apse*.

**EXPRESSIONISM**  A style at its peak *c.* 1920, more common on the Continent than in Britain, and seen more often in painting and sculpture than in architecture. At its most extreme it uses jagged or distorted forms, often creating a mood of anguish or unease.

**EXTRADOS**  Outer curved face of an *arch* or *vault*.

**EYECATCHER**  Decorative building terminating a vista.

**FAIENCE** (French): Moulded and fired glazed *terracotta* (clay ornament or *cladding*), when coloured or left white.

**FANLIGHT** A semicircular glazed opening, usually above a door, typical of *Georgian* architecture; sometimes used by extension for a rectangular glazed opening over a door.

**FAN-VAULT** A form of *vault* used after *c.* 1350, made up of halved concave masonry cones decorated with *blind tracery* [37].

**FASCIA** Plain horizontal band, e.g. in an *architrave*, or on a shopfront [23].

**FENESTRATION** The arrangement of windows in a façade.

**FERETORY** Site of the chief shrine of a church, behind the high altar.

**FERRAMENTA** Metal window grid to which glazing, especially stained glass, is secured.

**FESTOON** Ornamental garland, shown as if suspended from both ends. Compare *swag*.

**FIBREGLASS** Synthetic resin *reinforced* with glass fibre; also called glass-reinforced polyester (*GRP*). **GRC**: glass-reinforced *concrete*.

**FIELD** The central flat area within *panelling*, often slightly projecting (*raised and fielded* panelling) [24].

**FILLET** A narrow flat band running down a medieval *shaft* or along a *roll moulding*. It separates larger curved *mouldings* in *classical cornices*, *fluting* or *bases* [13, 23].

**FINIAL**  Topmost ornamental feature, usually a *spike*, e.g. above a *spire*, *gable* or *cupola*.

**FLAMBOYANT**  The latest phase of French *Gothic* architecture, with *flowing tracery*.

**FLARED HEADER**  A brick laid with its short end exposed and burnt to a darker shade, usually producing a patterned effect.

**FLASH LOCK**  (canals): Removable weir or similar device through which boats pass on a flush of water. Superseded by the *pound lock*.

**FLATTED**  (Scots): Divided into apartments.

**FLÈCHE**  (French, *lit.* arrow): Slender *spire* on the *ridge* of a roof. Also called a *spirelet*.

**FLEMISH BOND**  Brickwork with alternating *headers* (short ends) and *stretchers* (long sides) showing [6].

**FLEMISH GABLE**  A *gable* with curved sides crowned by a *pediment* [14]. Also called a *Dutch gable*.

**FLEURON**  Medieval carved flower or leaf ornament, often rectilinear [21].

**FLOWING TRACERY**  *Bar tracery* with uninterrupted flowing curves, typical of the 14th century; also called *curvilinear tracery*.

**FLUSHWORK**  Trimmed (*knapped*) flint used with dressed stone to form patterns.

**FLUTING**  Series of concave grooves (flutes), their common edges sharp (*arris*) or blunt (*fillet*) [23].

**FLYING BUTTRESS**  A *buttress* which transmits the thrust to a heavy support (*abutment*) by means of an *arch* or half-arch [7].

**FLYING STAIR**  A stair with one or more flights unsupported by a wall on either side.

**FOIL**  (*lit.* leaf): Lobe formed by the cusping of a circular or other shape in *tracery*. *Trefoil* (three), *quatrefoil* (four), *cinquefoil* (five), *sexfoil* (six) and *multifoil* express the number of lobes in a shape.

**FOLIATE**  Decorated with leaves.

**FONT**  Vessel in a church or chapel for baptismal water, usually of stone or lead.

**FORE-BUILDING**  Structure protecting an entrance.

**FORESTAIR**  External stair, usually unenclosed.

**FORMWORK** Also called falsework. Temporary framing of timber or metal used to support masonry arches during construction. Also used in casting *concrete*, when it is often called *shuttering*.

**FOSSE** A defensive ditch.

**FOUR-CENTRED ARCH** An *arch* with four arcs, the lower two curving inward more than the upper, with a blunt central point; typical of late medieval English architecture [3].

**FRAMED BUILDING** One in which the structure is carried by a framework – e.g. of steel, *reinforced concrete* or timber – instead of by load-bearing walls.

**FRANÇOIS I** The style of the early French *Renaissance* (Francis I, king 1515–47), marked especially by an all-over use of small-scale *classical* ornament.

**FRATER** The dining hall of an abbey or monastery, traditionally placed in the *cloister* range furthest from the church. Also called a *refectory*.

**FREE STYLE** Used for buildings of *c.* 1900 which eschew the use of any particular historical style, drawing instead on a mixture of (usually) late *Gothic*, *Renaissance* and *Art Nouveau* motifs.

**FREESTONE** Stone that is cut, or can be cut, in all directions.

**FRESCO** Painting on plaster. **AL FRESCO**: painting on wet plaster. **FRESCO SECCO**: painting on dry plaster.

**FRET** A geometrical ornament composed of a repeating pattern of horizontal and vertical lines or strips.

**FRIEZE** The middle member of the *classical entablature*, sometimes ornamented [23]. **PULVINATED FRIEZE** (*lit.* cushioned): of bold convex profile. Also a horizontal band of ornament.

**FRONTAL** Covering for the front of an altar.

**FRONTISPIECE** In 16th- and 17th-century buildings, the central feature of doorway and windows above linked in one composition.

**FROST-WORK** A form of *rustication* (the exaggerated treatment of masonry to give an effect of strength), treated like icicles or stalactites; also called *glaciation*.

**FULL CRUCK**   A type of timber construction in which
curving paired members (*blades*) rise from ground level
to the apex of the roof, serving as the main elements of
a roof *truss* [11].

**GABLE** Peaked external wall at the end of a double-pitch roof [14]. Types include: **DUTCH GABLE**, with curved sides crowned by a *pediment* (also called a **FLEMISH GABLE**); **KNEELERED GABLE**, with sides rising from projecting stones (*kneelers*); **PEDIMENTAL GABLE**, with *classical mouldings* along the top; **SHAPED GABLE**, with curved sides; **TUMBLED GABLE**, with *courses* or brick or stonework laid at right-angles to the slope. Also (Scots) a whole end wall, of whatever shape.

**GABLET** A small *gable* [14].

**GADROONING** *Classical* ribbed ornament like inverted *fluting* that flows into a lobed edge.

**GALILEE** Chapel or vestibule usually at the west end of a church and enclosing the main entrances.

**GALLERY** A long room or passage; an upper storey above the *aisles* of a church, looking through *arches* to the *nave*; a balcony or *mezzanine* overlooking the main interior space of a building; or an external walkway.

**GALLETING** Small stones set in a mortar *course*. See *cherry-caulking*.

**GAMBREL ROOF** A *hipped roof* which turns to a *gablet* at the *ridge* [14].

**GARDEROBE** A medieval privy; usually built into the thickness of an external wall.

**GARGOYLE** Projecting water spout often carved into human or animal shape.

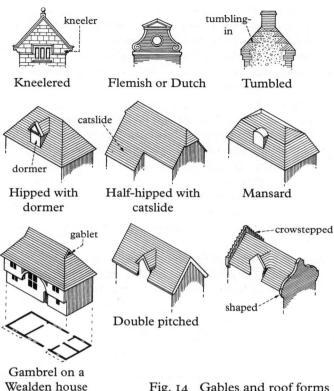

Fig. 14    Gables and roof forms

**GAUGED BRICKWORK**   Soft brick sawn roughly, then rubbed to a precise (gauged) surface. Mostly used for door or window openings [3]. Also called *rubbed brickwork*.

**GAZEBO**   (jocular Latin, 'I shall gaze'): Ornamental lookout tower or raised summerhouse.

**GEODESIC DOME**   A part-spherical structure of lightweight rods, joined in an even three-dimensional frame (called a space-frame), developed by the American engineer R. Buckminster Fuller (1895–1983).

**GEOMETRIC**   English *Gothic* architecture *c.* 1240–1290. During this period the French invention of *bar tracery* allowed for larger windows subdivided by stone *mullions* and *tracery*, in place of the single *lancets* of the *Early*

*English* style. Geometrical tracery is the earliest kind of this bar tracery, i.e. with patterns formed by intersecting moulded ribwork continuing upwards from the mullions, using simple forms, especially circles [4; pl. 6].

**GEOMETRICAL STAIR**  A stair *cantilevered* from the walls of the stairwell, without *newels*.

**GEORGIAN**  The architecture of the British Isles in the reigns of George I, II, III and IV, i.e. 1714–1830, in which the *classical* style and classical proportions became the norm for both major and minor buildings.

**GIANT ORDER**  In *classical* architecture, an *order* whose height is that of two or more storeys of the building to which it is applied. Also called a *colossal order*.

**GIB DOOR**  A concealed door, made flush with the wall surface and treated to resemble it; more often spelt *jib door*.

**GIBBS SURROUND**  An opening embellished with alternating or intermittent blocks, seen particularly in the work of James Gibbs (1682–1754) [15].

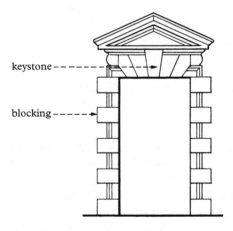

keystone

blocking

Fig. 15   Gibbs surround

**GIRDER**  A large beam. **BOX GIRDER**: of hollow-box section. **BOWED GIRDER**: with its top rising in an *arch*. **LATTICE GIRDER**: with *braced* framework. **PLATE GIRDER**: of I-section, made from iron or steel *plates*.

**GISANT**   In a monument, an effigy depicted as a naked corpse; also called a *cadaver*.

**GLACIATED**   Of masonry, carved in the form of icicles; hence e.g. glacial *quoins* [29]. Also called *frost-work*.

**GLACIS**   Artificial slope extending out and downwards from the *parapet* of a fort.

**GLAZING BARS**   Wooden or metal bars separating and supporting window panes.

**GNOMON**   Vane or indicator casting a shadow onto a sundial.

**GOTHIC**   The style of the Middle Ages from the later 12th century to the *Renaissance*, with which it co-existed in certain forms into the 17th century. Characterized in its full development by the pointed *arch*, the *rib-vault* and an often skeletal masonry structure for churches, combined with large glazed windows. The term was originally associated with the concept of the barbarian Goths as assailants of *classical* civilization.

**GOTHIC REVIVAL**   The self-conscious and often scrupulously accurate use of *Gothic* architecture for its historical or religious associations. It began in the 17th century and reached its peak in the 19th [pls 16, 18, 19, 20, 32].

**GOTHICK**   An early phase of the *Gothic Revival*, at its peak *c.* 1730–80, marked by thin, delicate forms used without much concern for *archaeological* accuracy or structural logic [pls 16, 18, 45].

**GRAFFITO** (plural: graffiti)   Scratched drawing or writing.

**GRANGE**   Farm owned and run by a religious order (a body or community of monks, nuns, etc.).

**GRC**   Glass-reinforced *concrete*.

**GREEK CROSS**   A cross with four arms of equal length.

**GREEK DORIC**   A version of the simplest and plainest of the three main *classical orders*, featuring a *frieze* with *triglyphs* and *metopes* [23]. A Greek Doric *column* has a thin spreading convex *capital* and no *base* to the column. Compare *Roman Doric*.

**GREEK FRET**   In *classical* architecture and decoration, a band of geometrical ornament composed of straight and vertical lines. Also called Greek key.

**GREEK REVIVAL**  The conscious revival of Greek *classical* architecture, as distinct from its later, *Roman* forms. At its peak in the early 19th century, its origins can be traced to the middle of the century before [pl. 46].

**GRISAILLE**  Monochrome painting, especially on walls or glass.

**GROIN**  Sharp edge at the meeting of two compartments (*cells*) of a *groin-vault* [37].

**GROIN-VAULT**  A *vault* formed of two *barrel vaults* intersecting at right angles [37].

**GROTESQUE**  (*lit.* grotto-esque): Wall decoration adopted from *Roman* examples in the *Renaissance*. Its foliage scrolls incorporate figurative elements. Compare *Arabesque*. Also used for a figure or head with distorted or unnatural features in medieval art and architecture.

**GROTTO**  Artificial cavern.

**GRP**  (glass-reinforced plastic): Synthetic resin *reinforced* with glass fibre; also called *fibreglass*.

**GUILLOCHE**  *Classical* ornament of *interlaced* bands [16].

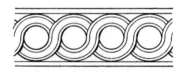

Fig. 16   Guilloche

**GUNLOOP**  Opening for a firearm [35].

**GUSHET**  (Scots): A triangular or wedge-shaped piece of land, or the corner building on such a site.

**GUTTAE**  Stylized drops below the *triglyphs* of the *frieze* in the *Doric order* of *classical* architecture [23].

**HAGIOSCOPE** An aperture in a wall or through a *pier* in a church or chapel, usually to allow a view of an altar. Also called a *squint*.

**HA-HA** A retaining wall sunk into a ditch in a landscape garden or park, used to make a barrier without disrupting the view.

**HALF-COLUMN** An *engaged column* half of whose circumference projects from the wall.

**HALF-HIPPED ROOF** A *gabled* roof with a sloped (hipped) end to the upper part only [14].

**HALF-TESTER** A *tomb-chest* with effigies beneath a flat canopy (*tester*) attached to a wall, with *columns* on one side only.

**HALF-TIMBERING** Archaic term for *timber framing*. Sometimes used for non-structural decorative timberwork.

**HALL-CHURCH** A church with *nave* and *aisles* of approximately equal height.

**HALL-KEEP** An early type of *keep* or principal tower in a castle, of rectangular plan, containing the great hall and chief bedchamber.

**HAMMERBEAMS** In a timber roof, horizontal *brackets* projecting at *wall-plate* level like an interrupted *tie-beam* [34]; the inner ends carry *hammerposts*, vertical timbers which support a *purlin* (horizontal longitudinal timber) and are *braced* to a *collar-beam* above.

**HAMMER-DRESSED**  Of *concrete*, textured with hammers after casting.

**HAMMERPOSTS**  In a hammerbeam roof, vertical timbers between the *hammerbeams* (horizontal *brackets* projecting at *wall-plate* level) and the *purlins* (horizontal longitudinal timbers); *braced* to a *collar-beam* above [34].

**HAMPER**  In 20th-century and later architecture, a visually distinct topmost storey or storeys.

**HARLING**  (Scots and Northern Irish; *lit.* hurling): Wet dash, i.e. a form of *roughcast rendering* in which the mixture of *aggregate* and binding material is dashed onto a wall.

**HATCHMENT**  A lozenge-shaped panel painted with armorial bearings, used in funeral ceremonies and often afterwards displayed in a church.

**HEADER**  A brick laid with its short end exposed [6]. A *flared header* is burnt to a darker shade, usually producing a patterned effect.

**HEADER BOND**  Brickwork with only the *headers* (short ends) of the bricks exposed.

**HEADSTOP**  A terminal to a *hoodmould* or *label* (projecting *moulding* above an *arch* or *lintel*) carved with a head [17].

**HELM ROOF**  A pyramidal roof set diagonally on a tower, so that it meets the walls by means of *gables* [7].

**HENGE**  Ritual earthwork.

**HERM**  (*lit.* the god Hermes): Male head or bust on a *pedestal*.

**HERRINGBONE WORK**  Bricks, tiles, stones or (sometimes) timbers laid diagonally, usually in superimposed alternate *courses* [34].

**HEXASTYLE**  Of a porch or *portico*: with six *columns* across the front.

**HIGH TECH**  A development of (especially) British Modernist architecture from the late 1960s, marked by the celebratory display of construction and services, a preference for lightweight materials and sheer surfaces, and a readiness to adopt new techniques from engineering and other technologies [pl. 36].

**HILL-FORT**  Earthwork of the *Iron Age* (*c.* 800–600 BC – 1st century AD) enclosed by a ditch and bank system.

**HIPPED ROOF**   A roof with sloped ends instead of *gables* [14].

**HOLLOW CHAMFER**   A *chamfer* (a surface formed by cutting off a square edge or corner) with a concave surface [8].

**HOODMOULD**   Projecting *moulding* above an *arch* or *lintel* to throw off water. When horizontal often called a *label* [4, 17].

headstop----▶                label stop----▶

Label

Fig. 17   Hoodmould

**HORSEMILL**   Circular or polygonal farm building with a central *shaft* turned by a horse to drive agricultural machinery.

**HUNGRY JOINTS**   Brick or stone joints without *pointing* (exposed mortar), or deeply recessed to show the outline of each stone.

**HUSK GARLAND**   A garland or *festoon* of stylized nutshells [18].

Fig. 18   Husk garland

**HYDRAULIC POWER**   Use of water under high pressure to work machinery.

**HYPOCAUST**   (*lit.* underburning): Roman heating system in which hot air was circulated under the floors.

# I

**ICONOSTASIS**  In Orthodox churches, the *screen* that divides off the *sanctuary*, usually decorated with sacred images (icons).

**IMPERIAL STAIR**  A stair rising in one flight and *returning* at right angles in two [32].

**IMPOST**  Horizontal *moulding* at the *springing* of an *arch* [3].

**IMPOST BLOCK**  On a *column*, a block between *abacus* and *capital*.

**IN ANTIS**  Of *classical columns*, set between *pilasters* or square columns of equal height, often within a *portico*.

**IN SITU**  Of *concrete*, cast in position on the building.

**INDENT**  Shape chiselled out of a stone to receive a monumental brass.

**INDUSTRIALIZED BUILDING**  System of manufactured units assembled on site. Also called *system building*.

**INFILL**  In timber-framed construction, the non-structural material that fills the compartments, e.g. wattle and daub, lath and plaster, brickwork (known as *nogging*), etc. [34].

**INGLENOOK**  (*lit.* fire-corner): Recess for a hearth with provision for seating.

**INGO**  (Scots): The *reveal* of a door or window opening where the stone is at right-angles to the wall.

**INTERCOLUMNIATION**  Interval between *columns*.

**INTERLACE** Decoration in relief simulating woven or entwined stems or bands. In *Norman* style architecture, a *frieze* of interconnecting *arches*.

**INTERSECTING TRACERY** A type of *bar tracery* used *c.* 1300, formed by interlocking *mullions* each branching out in two curved bars of the same radius but different centres [4].

**INTRADOS** Inner curve or underside of an *arch*.

**IONIC** One of the *orders* of *classical* architecture, distinguished in particular by downward- and inward-curling spirals (called *volutes*) on the *capital* of the *column* [23].

**IRON AGE** In Britain, the period from *c.* 800–600 B.C. to the coming of the Romans. Also used for those un-Romanized native communities which survived until the Saxon incursions, especially beyond the Roman frontiers.

**ITALIANATE** A style of *classical* secular architecture at its peak in the early to mid-19th century, derived from the palaces of *Renaissance* Italy, but often varied by asymmetrical elements [pls 29, 44].

**JACK ARCH** Shallow segmental *vault springing* from beams, used for fireproof floors, bridge decks, etc.

**JACOBEAN** The style of early 17th-century England, called after James I (reigned 1603–25), but common into the middle decades. Not always distinguishable from the preceding *Elizabethan* manner, with which it shares a fondness for densely applied *classical* ornament and symmetrical *gabled* façades.

**JACOBETHAN** A late-19th-century coinage for the revived *Elizabethan* or *Jacobean* styles.

**JAMB** (*lit.* leg): One of the vertical sides of an opening. Also (Scots) a wing or extension adjoining one side of a rectangular plan, making it into an L-, T- or Z-plan.

**JETTY** In a timber-framed building, the projection of an upper storey beyond the storey below, made by the beams and *joists* of the lower storey oversailing the wall [34]; on their outer ends is placed the *sill* of the walling for the storey above.

**JIB DOOR** A concealed door, made flush with the wall surface and treated to resemble it; sometimes spelt *gib door*.

**JOGGLE** The joining of two stones to prevent them slipping, by a notch in one and a projection in the other; hence joggling.

**JOINTED CRUCK** A type of timber construction in which the main supports or *blades* are formed from more than one timber [11]; the lower member may act as a *wall-post*; it is usually elbowed at *wall-plate* level and jointed just above.

**JOISTS** Horizontal timbers laid in parallel to support the floor of a building.

**KEEL MOULDING** *Moulding* used from the late 12th century, in section like the keel of a ship [21].

**KEEP** Principal tower of a castle.

**KENTISH CUSP** In *tracery* in the *Gothic* style, a cusp or curved projection which has a v-shaped opening set within the apex [4]. Also called a *split cusp*.

**KEY PATTERN** In *classical* architecture and decoration, a band of geometrical ornament composed of straight and vertical lines [19]. Also called *Greek fret* or Greek key.

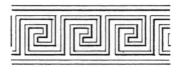

Fig. 19   Key pattern

**KEYSTONE** Central stone in an *arch* or *vault* [3, 15].

**KILLEEN** (Irish): A walled enclosure, often near old monastic sites, used until recent times for the burial of unbaptized children.

**KINGPOST** In a roof structure, a vertical timber set centrally on a *tie-beam*, rising to the apex of the roof to support a *ridge-piece* [34].

**KING-STRUT** In a roof structure, a vertical timber placed centrally on a *tie-beam*, not directly supporting longitudinal timbers. Compare *queen-strut*.

**KNAPPED** Of flint, worked to a flat outer surface.

**KNEELER** Horizontal projecting stone at the *base* of each side of a *gable* to support the inclined *coping* stones. A gable so formed is called a kneelered gable [14].

# L

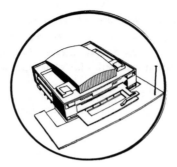

**LABEL**  Projecting horizontal *moulding* above an *arch* or *lintel* to throw off water [17]; also called a *hoodmould*.

**LABEL STOP**  An ornamental projection or *boss* at the end of a *label* or *hoodmould* [17].

**LACED BRICKWORK**  Vertical strips of brickwork, often in a contrasting colour, linking openings on different floors.

**LACING COURSE**  Horizontal reinforcement in timber or brick to walls of flint, cobble, etc.

**LADE**  (Scots): Channel formed to bring water to a mill; mill-race.

**LADY CHAPEL**  A chapel dedicated to the Virgin Mary (Our Lady).

**LAIR**  (Scots): A burial space reserved in a graveyard.

**LAIRD'S LOFT**  (Scots): A *gallery* in a church reserved for an individual or special group, when it is sometimes called a *trades loft*.

**LANCET**  Slender single-*light*, pointed-arched window [26]. Hence lancet style, the first phase of English *Gothic* architecture (*c.* 1180–1250; also called *Early English*), from its use of such windows.

**LANTERN**  Circular or polygonal windowed turret crowning a roof or a dome. Also the windowed stage of a *crossing tower* lighting a church interior.

**LANTERN CROSS**  Churchyard cross with lantern-shaped top.

**LATTICE GIRDER**  A *girder* with *braced* framework.

**LAVATORIUM**  In an abbey or monastery, a washing place adjacent to the *refectory* or dining hall.

**LEAN-TO**  A single sloping roof built against a vertical wall; also applied to the part of the building beneath. See *penthouse*.

**LEDGER SLAB**  A monolithic slab laid flat over a grave or tomb.

**LESENE**  (*lit.* a mean thing): A *pilaster* without *base* or *capital*. Also called a pilaster strip.

**LIERNES**  Short decorative ribs in the upper part of a *vault*, not linked to any *springing* point, and having no structural function; hence lierne vault [37].

**LIGHT**  Compartment of a window defined by the uprights or *mullions*.

**LIMEWASHING**  A method of painting walls with layers of very dilute lime putty. Internally, can have a disinfectant effect; externally, can help protect friable stone or soft bricks from *weathering*.

**LINENFOLD**  *Tudor panelling* carved with simulations of folded linen.

**LINTEL**  Horizontal beam or stone bridging an opening [3].

**LOFT**  A upper room or floor, especially within a roof space; also, a *gallery* in a church.

**LOGGIA**  (Italian): A *gallery* or room with regular openings along one main side, sometimes free-standing.

**LONG-AND-SHORT WORK**  Stones (*quoins*) at the angle or corner of a building placed with the long side alternately upright and horizontal, especially in *Anglo-Saxon* structures.

**LONGHOUSE**  House and byre in the same range with internal access between them. In the Yorkshire Dales, known as a laithe house.

**LOOPHOLE**  An unglazed slit window. Compare *arrow loop*.

**LOUIS XIV, LOUIS XV, LOUIS XVI**  The prevailing styles of French architecture for most of the 17th and 18th centuries (Louis XIV, king 1643–1715, Louis XV, 1715–74, Louis XVI, 1774–92). In British terminology, commonly used for the revival of the styles in the 19th and 20th centuries, especially for interiors.

**LOUVRE**  Roof opening, often protected by a raised timber structure, to allow the smoke from a central hearth to escape; also one of a series of horizontal boards or slats set at angle to prevent rain entering an opening.

**LOWSIDE WINDOW**  A side window set lower than the others in the *chancel* of a church, usually towards its west end.

**LUCAM**  Projecting housing for a hoist pulley on an upper storey of warehouses, mills, etc., for raising goods to the loading doors.

**LUCARNE**  Small *gabled* opening in a roof or *spire*.

**LUCKENBOOTH**  (Scots): Lock-up booth or shop.

**LUGGED**  Of an *architrave* (a formalized *lintel*), with side projections at the top [20]. Also called an *eared* architrave.

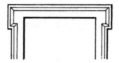

Fig. 20  Lugged architrave

**LUNETTE**  Semicircular window or blind panel.

**LYCHGATE**  (*lit.* corpse-gate): Roofed gateway entrance to a churchyard for the reception of a coffin.

**LYNCHET**  Long terraced strip of soil on the downward side of prehistoric and medieval fields, accumulated because of repeated ploughing along the contours.

23. *Norman*: Castle Hedingham, the keep, *c.* 1142. *Essex*

24. *Perpendicular*: Manchester, Chetham's School and Library, cloister, 1420s. *Lancashire: Manchester and the South-East*

25. *Timber framing*: Thaxted, Guildhall, third quarter of the C15, altered in 1715 and by Ernest Beckwith in 1910–11. *Essex*

26. *Tudor*: Beamsley Hospital, founded 1593. *Yorkshire West Riding: Leeds, Bradford and the North*

27. *Baroque*: Abingdon, County Hall, 1678–83, builder Christopher Kempster. *Berkshire*

28. *Baroque*: Stydd, almshouses, s front, 1728. *Lancashire: North*

29. *Italianate*: Perth, St John Street, Nos 48–50 (former Central Bank of Scotland), by David Rhind, 1846–7. *Perth and Kinross*

30. *Classical*: Liverpool, St George's Hall, the Concert Hall, 1850. *Liverpool City Guide*

31. *Classical*: Leeds
    Town Hall, Head-
    row, by Cuthbert
    Brodrick, 1852–8.
    *Leeds City Guide*

32. *Gothic Revival*:
    Liverpool, Victoria
    Building, University
    of Liverpool, by
    Alfred Waterhouse,
    1889–92. *Lancashire:
    Liverpool and the
    South-West*

33. *Modernist / Art Deco*:
    Morecambe, Mid-
    land Hotel, by Oliver
    Hill, 1932–3, E side.
    *Lancashire: North*

34. *Modernist*: London,
    The Economist
    Group, St James's
    Street, 1962–4 by
    Alison and Peter
    Smithson. *London 6:
    Westminster*

35. *Postmodernist*: London, Storm Water Pumping Station, Isle of Dogs, 1987–8, by John Outram. *London 5: East*

36. *Modernist* (*High Tech*): Gateshead, Sage Music Centre, Oakwellgate, 1996–2004, by Foster and Partners. *Newcastle and Gateshead City Guide*

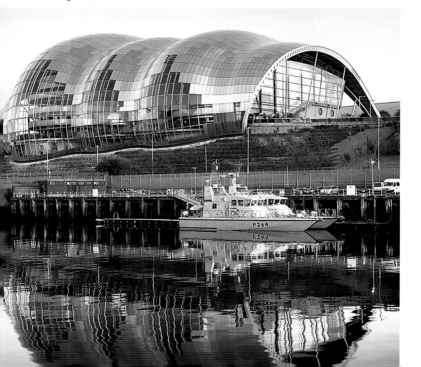

37. *Decorated*: Markenfield Hall, hall block, *c.* 1290–1310.
*Yorkshire West Riding: Leeds, Bradford and the North*

38. *Perpendicular*: Much Wenlock, Wenlock Priory, prior's lodging
range from the w, late 1420s, wall perhaps rebuilt *c.* 1500.
*Shropshire*

39. *Timber framing*: Bramley, Manor House, exterior, *c.* 1545–6.
    *Hampshire: Winchester and the North*

40. *Elizabethan*: Fountains Hall, attributed to Robert Smythson,
    *c.* 1600. *Yorkshire West Riding: Leeds, Bradford and the North*

41. *Palladian*: Hagley Hall, 1754–60, by Sanderson Miller. *Worcestershire*

42. *Rococo*: Lytham Hall, staircase hall, plasterwork by Giuseppe Cortese, *c.* 1764. *Lancashire: North*

52. *Modernist*: Ulting, The Studio, by Richard & Su Rogers, 1968–9. *Essex*

53. *Modernist*: Nolton, Malator, by Future Systems, 1998. *Pembrokeshire*

**MACHICOLATIONS** (*lit.* mashing devices): On a castle, a series of openings between the *corbels* that support a projecting *parapet* through which missiles can be dropped. Used decoratively on post-medieval buildings [35].

**MAINS** (Scots): Home farm on an estate.

**MANNERISM** The predominant style of mid- to late-16th-century Italy, in which *classical* motifs may be used in deliberate disregard of original conventions or contexts; by extension, a self-consciously formal approach to design in other idioms. The decorative classical architecture of mid-17th-century England is sometimes called *Artisan Mannerism*, because master masons and other craftsmen were its chief exponents.

**MANOMETER TOWER** A tower containing a *column* of water to regulate pressure in water mains. Also called a *standpipe tower*.

**MANSARD** A roof of two pitches, the upper one less steep than the lower [14].

**MANSE** (chiefly Scots): House of a minister of religion.

**MARGINS** (chiefly Scots): Dressed stones at the edges of an opening. Also called *rybats*.

**MARRIAGE LINTEL** (Scots): *Lintel* carved with the initials of the owner and his wife and the date of building work (only coincidentally of their marriage).

**MATHEMATICAL TILES** Facing tiles with the appearance of brick, most often applied to timber-framed walls.

**MATRIX** The setting of a brass or other inlaid material.

**MAUSOLEUM** Monumental building or chamber usually intended for the burial of members of one family.

**MEGALITHIC** The use of large stones, singly or together.

**MEGALITHIC TOMB** Massive stone-built burial chamber of the new Stone Age covered by an earth or stone mound.

**MERCAT** (Scots): Market. The mercat cross, which is topped more often by a heraldic or other *finial* rather than a cross, was the focus of market activity and local ceremonial.

**MERLONS** The solid uprights of a *battlement* [35].

**METOPES** The spaces between the *triglyphs* in a *Doric frieze*, often ornamented with sculpture [23].

**MEZZANINE** Low storey between two higher ones.

**MIDDLE CRUCK** A type of timber construction in which the upper supports or *blades* rise from halfway up the walls to a *tie-beam* or *collar-beam*, rather than continuing up to the apex.

**MILD STEEL** An easily workable steel, with good tensile strength, used increasingly since the mid-19th century as a cheaper substitute for *wrought iron*.

**MINIMALISM** A term adopted from painting and sculpture for a tendency within Modernist architecture from the 1980s onwards towards simple forms and volumes, typified by the all-white interior.

**MISERICORD** (*lit.* mercy): Shelf on a carved *bracket* placed on the underside of a hinged *choir stall* seat to support a standing occupant.

**MITRE** In joinery, the meeting of two members of identical section at a diagonal.

**MIXER-COURTS** Forecourts to groups of houses shared by vehicles and pedestrians.

**MODERNISM** The single most important new style or philosophy of design of the 20th century, associated with an analytical approach to the function of buildings, a strictly rational use of (often new) materials, an openness to structural innovation and the elimination of ornament. The Modern Movement is a narrower term, used in Britain for the rigorous Modernist architecture of the period *c.* 1930–55, after which it becomes hard to distinguish from ordinary building in non-traditional styles [pls 22, 33, 34, 36, 52, 53].

**MODILLIONS** Small *brackets* or *consoles* along the underside of a *Corinthian* or *Composite cornice*. Often also used on an *eaves* cornice [23].

**MODULE** A predetermined standard size for co-ordinating the dimensions of components of a building; hence modular planning, etc. In *classical* architecture, the module is usually a multiple or fraction of the width of the *order* or type of *column* used.

**MORT-SAFE** (Scots): Device to secure corpse(s): either in an iron frame over a grave or a building where bodies were kept during decomposition.

**MOTTE-AND-BAILEY** Post-Roman and *Norman* defence consisting of an earthen mound (motte) topped by a wooden tower within a *bailey*, an enclosure defended by a ditch and palisade, and also, sometimes, by an internal bank.

**MOUCHETTE** A curved *dagger*-shaped motif in *tracery*, popular especially in the 14th century [4].

**MOULDING** Shaped ornamental strip of continuous section, e.g. the *classical cavetto*, *cyma* or *ovolo* [21, 23].

**MULLION** Vertical member between window *lights* [4].

**MULTIFOIL** In *tracery*, with multiple lobes (*foils*) formed by the cusping of a circular or curved shape.

**MULTI-STOREY** Of five or more storeys.

**MULTIVALLATE** Of a hillfort: defended by three or more concentric banks and ditches.

**MUNTIN** The vertical part in the framing of a door, screen or (especially) *panelling* [24].

**MURDER HOLE** Small rectangular trap in the ceiling of an entrance passage in a castle or *tower house*.

**MUTULES** Square blocks attached to the underside of a *Doric cornice*, in line with the *triglyphs*.

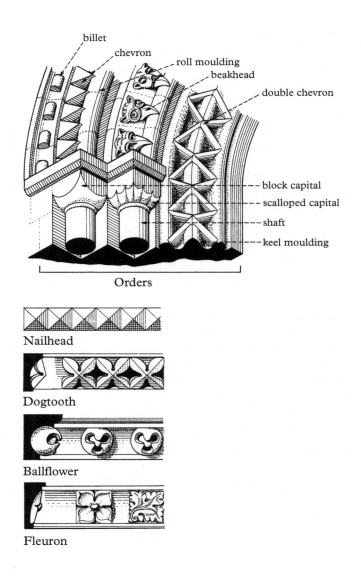

billet

chevron

roll moulding

beakhead

double chevron

block capital

scalloped capital

shaft

keel moulding

Orders

Nailhead

Dogtooth

Ballflower

Fleuron

Fig. 21 Moulding and ornament

**NAILHEAD** Ornament in the *Early English* period of *Gothic*, consisting of small pyramids regularly repeated [21].

**NAOS** The space within a *classical* temple [27]. Also called a *cella*.

**NARTHEX** Enclosed vestibule or covered porch at the main entrance to a church.

**NAVE** The body of a church west of the *crossing* or *chancel*, often flanked by *aisles*.

**NEEDLE SPIRE** A thin *spire* rising from the centre of a tower roof, well inside the *parapet*.

**NEO-BAROQUE** The revival of the *Baroque* style, especially in early 20th-century Britain; also termed Edwardian Baroque. It tended to look back to English prototypes of the late 17th and early 18th centuries rather than to the more expansive models of the Continent, where *Baroque* architecture originated.

**NEO-BYZANTINE** The revival in the late 19th and early 20th centuries of the *Byzantine* style associated with Eastern or Orthodox Christianity, which originated at Byzantium (Constantinople) in the 5th century. Characterized by round *arches*, *vaults* and domes, ornament of emblematic and symbolic significance, and the use of mosaic [pl. 21].

**NEO-CLASSICISM** A tendency within *classical* architecture, at its peak in the late 18th and early 19th centuries,

85

which aimed at a purer imitation of the buildings of the Greeks and Romans, or at a more logical and rigorous use of the elements of the classical style [pls 17, 43].

**NEO-GEORGIAN** The revival of the British and Irish architecture of the 18th and early 19th centuries. It often depends for its effects on *sash windows*, symmetry, and carefully calculated proportions rather than on displays of *columns* and grand formal features. At its peak in the 1920s, it can be traced back to the late 19th century and is still current, often in a debased form, as a style mostly for private houses.

**NEOLITHIC** New Stone Age in Britain, *c.* 3500 B.C. until the *Bronze Age*, *c.* 2000 B.C.

**NEO-RENAISSANCE** The *classical* manner of the 15th to the 17th centuries, especially that of Italy, as revived in the 19th century and later.

**NEO-VERNACULAR** A tendency within (especially) 20th-century architecture, at its strongest since the 1970s, which seeks to evoke local traditions of building, usually in pursuit of a friendly, domestic image.

**NEO-WREN** A style of the late 19th and early 20th centuries, based on the works of the English *Baroque* architect Sir Christopher Wren (1632–1723) and his contemporaries. Sometimes facetiously called *Wrenaissance*.

**NEWEL** Central or corner *post* of a staircase [32]. A newel stair ascends round a central supporting newel; in Scotland called a turnpike stair.

**NIGHT STAIR** Stair from the dormitory into the *transept* of an abbey or monastery church, used for entry to night services.

**NODDING OGEE** An *ogee* or double-curved pointed *arch* that also projects forward at the top.

**NOGGING** Brickwork *infilling* of a timber-framed wall [34].

**NOOK-SHAFT** *Shaft* set in the angle of a wall or opening [13].

**NORMAN** The English version of the *Romanesque* style, which predominated in Western Europe in the 11th and 12th centuries; so called because it was propagated after the Norman Conquest in 1066. It is associated especially with the expansion of monasticism and the building of large stone churches, and is characterized by massive masonry, round-headed *arches* and *vaulting* inspired by ancient *Roman* precedent, and by the use of stylized ornament [pls 2, 3, 23].

**NOSING**   Projection of the *tread* of a step [32].

**NUTMEG**   Medieval ornament with a chain of tiny triangles placed obliquely.

**OBELISK** Lofty *pillar* of square section, tapering at the top and ending pyramidically.

**OCTOSTYLE** Of a porch or *portico*: with eight *columns* across the front.

**OCULUS** Circular opening [22].

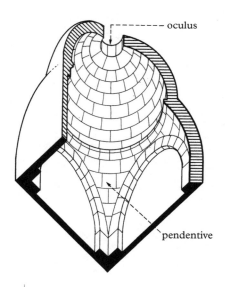

Fig. 22 Oculus and pendentive (in a dome)

**OEIL DE BOEUF** Small oval window, set horizontally. Also called a *bullseye window*.

**OGEE** A double curve, bending first one way and then the other. An *ogee* or ogival *arch*, especially popular in the 14th century, is pointed at the top [3]. A *nodding ogee* curves forward from the wall face at the top.

**OLD ENGLISH** A style used from *c.* 1860, in which *tile-hanging*, tall chimneys, *half-timbering* and other details of the *gabled vernacular* architecture of south-east England are picturesquely combined [pl. 48].

**OPEN PEDIMENT** A *pediment* with the centre of the *base* omitted [25].

**OPEN STRING** A sloping member of a staircase covering the ends of the *treads* and *risers* and cut into their shape [32]; hence an open string staircase. Compare *closed string*.

**OPUS SECTILE** Decorative mosaic-like facing.

**OPUS SIGNINUM** Composition flooring of Roman origin.

**ORATORY** A private chapel in a church or house. Also a church of the Oratorians (Roman Catholic).

**ORDER** One of a series of recessed *arches* and *jambs* forming a *splayed* medieval opening, e.g. a doorway or *arcade* arch [21]. Also, an upright structural member used in series, especially in *classical* architecture: see *Orders*.

**ORDERS** The differently formalized versions of the basic *post*-and-*lintel* (*column* and *entablature*) system in *classical* architecture. The main orders are *Doric, Ionic,* and *Corinthian*. They are Greek in origin but occur in *Roman* versions. *Tuscan* is a simple variant of *Roman Doric*. The *Composite capital* combines Ionic *volutes* with Corinthian foliage. Though each order has its own conventions of design and proportion, there are many minor variations [23]. **SUPERIMPOSED ORDERS**: orders on successive levels, customarily in the upward sequence of Tuscan, Doric, Ionic, Corinthian, Composite.

**ORGAN LOFT** In a church, a *gallery* in which the organ is placed.

**ORIEL** A *bay window* which rests on *corbels* or *brackets* and starts above ground level.

**OVERARCH** An *arch* framing an opening in a wall, e.g. a window or door.

89

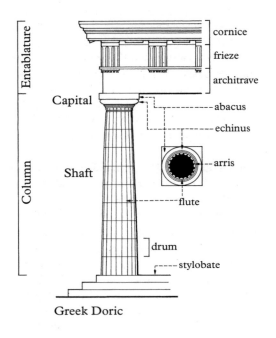

cornice

frieze

architrave

Entablature

Capital

abacus

echinus

Column

Shaft

arris

flute

drum

stylobate

Greek Doric

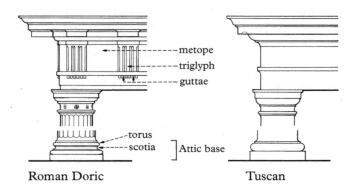

metope

triglyph

guttae

torus

scotia

Attic base

Roman Doric

Tuscan

Fig. 23   Orders

90

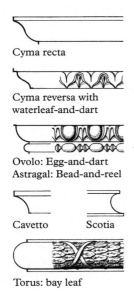

Cyma recta

Cyma reversa with
waterleaf-and-dart

Ovolo: Egg-and-dart
Astragal: Bead-and-reel

Cavetto          Scotia

Torus: bay leaf

## Mouldings and Enrichments

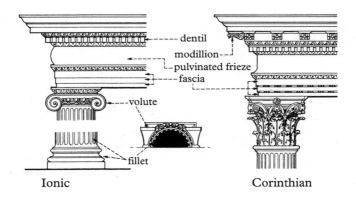

dentil

modillion--
--pulvinated frieze
fascia

volute

fillet

Ionic                    Corinthian

**OVERDOOR**  Painting or relief above an internal door. Also called a *sopraporta*.

**OVERMANTEL**  An ornamented or painted feature above a fireplace.

**OVERSHOT WATER WHEEL**  One with water fed on to the wheel over the top. The wheel thus revolves anti-clockwise. Compare *breastshot*, *pitchback* and *undershot*.

**OVERTHROW**  Decorative fixed *arch* between two gatepiers or above a gate, often of iron.

**OVOLO**  Wide convex *moulding* [23].

**PALAZZO** (Italian, palace): used for any compact and ornate building like a large Italian town house, usually *classical* in style.

**PALIMPSEST** (*lit.* scraped again): Reuse of a surface. Of a brass: where a metal *plate* has been reused by turning over and engraving on the back. Of a wall painting: where one overlaps and partly obscures an earlier one.

**PALLADIAN** Derived from the buildings and publications of the Italian *classical* architect Andrea Palladio (1508–80). His manner was introduced to Britain by Inigo Jones in the early 17th century, and was revived by Lord Burlington and others in the 18th century, in both cases as a counter to the less strict or pure styles of the day. Its influence continued well into the 19th century [pl. 41].

**PALLADIAN WINDOW** In *classical* architecture, a window with an arched central *light* flanked by two lower straight-headed ones; the motif is also used for other openings. Also called *Serlian window*, Serlian motif, Serliana, and *Venetian window*.

**PALMETTE** *Classical* ornament like a symmetrical palm shoot [2].

**PANEL FRAME** (Scots): Moulded stone frame round an armorial panel, often placed over the entrance to a *tower house* [35].

**PANEL TRACERY** *Bar tracery* with even upright divisions made by a horizontal *transom* or transoms [4].

**PANELLING** Wooden lining to interior walls, made up of vertical members (*muntins*) and horizontals (*rails*) framing panels [24]; also called *wainscot*. **RAISED AND FIELDED**: with the central area of the panel (*field*) raised up. Also used for stonework treated with sunk or raised panels.

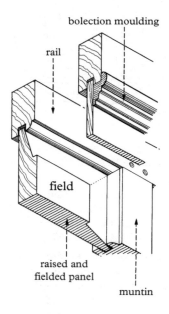

Fig. 24   Panelling

**PANTILE**   Roof tile of curved S-shaped section.

**PANTRY**   In a medieval house or college, a room off the *screens passage*, used for storing provisions; compare *buttery*.

**PARABOLIC ARCH**   An *arch* shaped like a chain suspended from two level points, but inverted [3].

**PARAPET**   Wall for protection at any sudden drop, e.g. on a bridge, or at the *wallhead* of a castle where it protects the *parapet* walk or *wall-walk*. Also used to conceal a roof.

**PARCHEMIN PANEL**   With a vertical central rib or *moulding* branching in *ogee* curves to meet the four corners of the panel. Sometimes used with *linenfold panelling*.

**PARCLOSE SCREEN** A *screen* separating a chapel from the rest of the church.

**PARGETING** (*lit.* plastering): Exterior plaster decoration, either moulded in relief or incised.

**PARLOUR** In an abbey or monastery, a room where talking was permitted; in a medieval house, the semi-private living room below the *solar* or upper chamber.

**PARTERRE** Level space in a garden laid out with low, formal beds of plants.

**PASSING BRACES** Long straight *braces* in a timber roof, passing across other members of the *truss*.

**PATENT GLAZING** Large-paned glazing with minimal framing, developed in the 20th century.

**PATERA** (*lit.* plate): Round or oval *classical* ornament in shallow relief.

**PATTE D'OIE** (French, *lit.* goose foot): A feature in garden design in which three radiating avenues focus on a single point; derived from French *Baroque* layouts.

**PAVILION** Ornamental building for occasional use in a garden, park, etc.; or a projecting subdivision of a larger building, often at an angle or terminating a wing.

**PEBBLEDASHING** A form of wall covering in which pebbles or gravel are thrown at the wet plaster for a textured effect.

**PEDESTAL** A tall block carrying a *classical column*, statue, vase, etc.

**PEDIMENT** A formalized *gable* derived from that of a *classical* temple; also used over doors, windows etc. [25]. A **BROKEN PEDIMENT** has its apex omitted. An **OPEN PEDIMENT** has the centre of the *base* omitted. A broken pediment with double-curved sides is called a **SWAN-NECK PEDIMENT**.

**PEDIMENTAL GABLE** A segmental or shallow triangular *gable* treated as a *pediment*, i.e. with *classical mouldings* along the top.

**PEEL TOWER, PELE TOWER** Small defensible tower or *tower house* of stone, especially near the Scottish-English border.

**PEND** (Scots): Open-ended ground-level passage through a building.

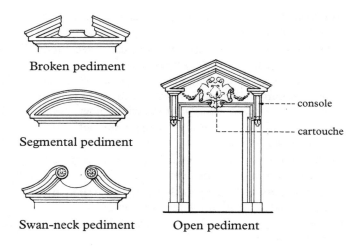

Broken pediment

Segmental pediment

Swan-neck pediment

Open pediment

---- console

---- cartouche

Fig. 25   Pediments

**PENDANT**   An ornamental feature suspended from a ceiling or *vault*.

**PENDENTIVE**   The surface between *arches* that meet at an angle, formed as part of a hemisphere and supporting a *drum*, dome or *vault* [22].

**PENTHOUSE**   Subsidiary structure with a *lean-to* roof. Also a separately roofed structure on top of a *multi-storey* block of the 20th century or later.

**PEPPERPOT TURRET**   A *corbelled* turret or *bartizan*, square or round, frequently at an angle.

**PERIPTERAL**   Of a temple: with a *colonnade* all round the exterior.

**PERISTYLE**   On a *classical* building, a *colonnade* all round the exterior or an interior space, e.g. a courtyard.

**PERPENDICULAR**   English version of late *Gothic*, developed from the 1320s, which continued into the early 16th century; sometimes abbreviated to Perp. Characterised by large windows with a grid pattern of *mullions* and *transoms*, with the mullions continuing to the head to the *arch*, which is often of flattened or four-centred form. This motif of *panel tracery* is used also for wall decoration, and on the fan *vaults* that were used for the most prestigious buildings [pls 10, 12, 13, 24, 38].

**PERRON**  Central stair to a doorway, usually of double-curved plan.

**PEW**  Loosely, seating for the laity outside the *chancel*; strictly, an enclosed seat. A **BOX PEW** is enclosed by a high wooden back and ends, the latter having doors. **CHURCHWARDEN'S PEW**: an especially tall or elaborate pew for use by the churchwarden, usually placed at the west end of a church.

**PIANO NOBILE**  (Italian): Principal floor of a *classical* building, above a ground floor or *basement* and with a lesser storey overhead.

**PIAZZA**  Formal urban open space surrounded by buildings.

**PICTURESQUE**  An approach to architecture and landscape design first defined by English theorists in the later 18th century. Characterized in architecture by irregular forms and textures, sometimes with the implication of gradual growth or decay, and in planning by a preference for asymmetrical layouts that composed into attractive views. Its influence continued into the 20th century, for instance in the arrangement of some post-war New Towns [pls 44, 47].

**PIENDED ROOF**  The Scottish term for a *hipped roof*, with sloping rather than *gabled* ends. A piended platform roof is flat in the centre.

**PIER**  Large masonry or brick support, often for an *arch*. A *compound pier* is composed of grouped *shafts*, or a solid core surrounded by shafts.

**PIETRA DURA**  (Italian, *lit.* hard stone): Ornamental or pictorial inlay by means of thin slabs of stone.

**PILASTER**  Flat representation of a *classical column* in shallow relief. A pilaster *respond* is set at the end of a *colonnade*, *arcade* etc. to balance visually the column which it faces. A pilaster strip is a pilaster without *base* or *capital* (also called a *lesene*).

**PILASTRADE**  A series of *pilasters* or flat representation of *classical columns*, equivalent to a *colonnade*.

**PILE**  Row of rooms. The most common use of the term is in *double pile*, describing a building, especially a house, that is two rooms deep.

**PILLAR** Free-standing upright member of any section, not conforming to one of the *classical orders*.

**PILLAR PISCINA** In a church or chapel, a free-standing basin (*piscina*) for washing Mass vessels.

**PILOTIS** (French): 20th-century term for *pillars* or stilts that support a building above an open ground floor.

**PINNACLE** A small *spike*- or turret-like termination of a *buttress*, *parapet* etc., especially in *Gothic* architecture.

**PINS OR PINNING** (Scots): Lines of tiny stones used decoratively in the mortar joints. See *cherry-caulking* and *galleting*.

**PISCINA** In a church or chapel, a basin for washing Mass vessels, provided with a drain, usually set in or against the wall to the south of an altar.

**PISÉ** Walling material of clay mixed with straw. Also called *cob* and, in North Cumberland, clay dabbin.

**PIT PRISON** (Scots): Sunk chamber with access from above through a hatch.

**PITCHBACK WATER WHEEL** One with water fed on to the wheel just behind top centre, thus turning the wheel clockwise. Compare *breastshot*, *overshot* and *undershot*.

**PITCHED MASONRY** Laid on the diagonal, often alternately with opposing *courses* (pitched and counterpitched, also called *herringbone*).

**PLACE BRICKS** The poorer kind of bricks, used on internal or concealed construction. Compare *stock bricks*.

**PLATBAND** Flat plain horizontal *course* or *moulding* between storeys.

**PLATE** Longitudinal member of a timber-framed building, set square to the ground.

**PLATE GIRDER** A *girder* of I-section, made from iron or steel *plates*.

**PLATE RAIL** On a railway, an L-section *rail* for plain unflanged wheels. Compare *edge rail*.

**PLATE TRACERY** The earliest form of *tracery*, introduced *c.* 1200, in which shapes are cut through solid masonry [26].

**PLATEWAY** Early railway using *plate rails*, i.e. *rails* of L-section (compare *edge rails*).

**PLATT** (Scots): Platform, doorstep or landing.

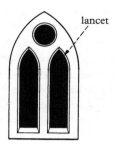

Fig. 26  Plate tracery

**PLEASANCE**  (Scots): *Close* or walled garden.

**PLINTH**  Projecting *courses* at the foot of a wall or *column*, generally cut back (*chamfered*) or moulded at the top.

**POCKED TOOLING**  *Hammer-dressed* stonework with a pocked appearance, characteristic of Irish masonry from the 14th to the 16th centuries.

**PODIUM**  A continuous raised platform supporting a building; or a large block of two or three storeys beneath a *multi-storey* block of smaller area.

**POINT BLOCK**  A *multi-storey* block with flats fanning out from a central core of lifts, staircases etc.

**POINTING**  Exposed mortar jointing of masonry or brickwork. It can be flush or recessed. *Bag-rubbed pointing* is flush at the edges and gently recessed in the middle. Bucket-handle pointing is formed with a round stick or curved tool to emphasise the recess. *Ribbon pointing* has joints formed with a trowel so that they stand out (and accelerate the decay of the masonry). **TUCK POINTING**: the mortar is usually coloured to match the brick, but has a narrow central channel filled with finer, whiter mortar, thus simulating more closely-laid brickwork.

**POPPYHEAD**  Carved ornament of leaves and flowers as a termination or *finial* on top of a bench end or *stall*.

**PORTAL FRAME**  A single-storey frame used from the 20th century, comprising two uprights rigidly connected to a beam or pair of *rafters*, particularly to support a roof.

**PORTCULLIS** Gate constructed to rise and fall in vertical grooves at the entry to a castle.

**PORTE COCHÈRE** (French, *lit.* gate for coaches): Porch large enough to admit wheeled vehicles.

**PORTICO** A porch with the roof and frequently a *pediment* supported by a row of *columns* [27]. Porticoes are described by the number of columns, e.g. *distyle* (two), *tetrastyle* (four), *hexastyle* (six), *octostyle* (eight). A *prostyle* portico has columns standing free. A portico in antis has columns on the same plane as the front of the building. **BLIND PORTICO**: the front features of a portico applied to a wall; also called a *temple front*.

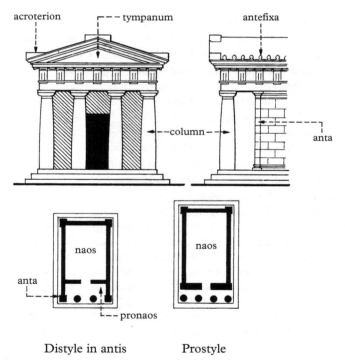

Distyle in antis          Prostyle

Fig. 27 Portico

**PORTICUS** (plural: porticus)   Subsidiary room or *cell* opening from the main body of an *Anglo-Saxon* church.

**PORTLAND STONE**   A hard, durable white limestone from the Isle of Portland in Dorset. Portland *roach* is rough-textured and has small cavities and fossil shells.

**POST**   Upright support in a structure [34].

**POSTERN**   Small gateway at the back of a building, especially a castle or gatehouse, or to the side of a larger entrance door or gate.

**POSTMODERNISM**   A much-debated cultural label, used in the architectural world since the 1970s to denote the reuse of motifs from historical styles, in contexts where a Modernist approach would have omitted them. Postmodern buildings often mix these in a knowing or ironical way, sometimes in combination with new materials and for non-traditional functions [pl. 35].

**POTENCE**   (Scots): Rotating ladder for access to nesting boxes in a *doocot* (dovecote).

**POUND LOCK**   (canals): A chamber with gates at each end allowing boats to float from one level to another. Successor to the *flash lock*.

**PRE-CAST**   Of *concrete*: cast as components before construction.

**PREDELLA**   In an *altarpiece*, the horizontal strip below the main representation, often used for subsidiary representations.

**PREFABRICATION**   Manufacture of buildings or components off-site for assembly on-site.

**PRESBYTERY**   The part of a church lying east of the *choir* where the main altar is placed. Also a priest's residence.

**PRE-STRESSED**   Of *concrete*: incorporating tensioned steel rods.

**PRINCIPALS**   In a roof, a pair of inclined lateral timbers or *rafters* of a *truss*. Usually they support horizontal side timbers called *purlins*, and mark the main *bay* divisions [34].

**PRONAOS**   The space within the *portico* of a *classical* temple [27].

**PROSTYLE**   Of a porch or *portico*: with *columns* standing free [27].

**PULPIT**   Raised and enclosed platform for the preaching of sermons. **THREE-DECKER**: with reading desk below and clerk's desk below that. **TWO-DECKER**: as above, minus the clerks' desk.

**PULPITUM**   Stone *screen* in a major church dividing *choir* from *nave*. In monastic churches, separating the monks from the laity.

**PULVINATED**   (*lit.* cushioned): Of a *frieze*: of bold convex profile [23].

**PURBECK**   A dark limestone from Purbeck in Dorset, which can be polished; used especially in the first two centuries of English *Gothic* architecture.

**PURLIN**   Horizontal longitudinal timber in a roof structure [34]. **COLLAR PURLIN** or **CROWN PLATE**: central timber which carries *collar-beams* and is supported by *crown-posts*. **SIDE PURLINS**: pairs of timbers placed some way up the slope of the roof, which carry *common rafters*. **BUTT PURLINS** or **TENONED PURLINS** are tenoned into either side of the *principals*. **THROUGH PURLINS** pass through or past the principal; they include **CLASPED PURLINS**, which rest on *queenposts* or are carried in the angle between principals and *collar*, and **TRENCHED PURLINS** which are trenched into the backs of principals.

**PUTLOG HOLES**   Holes in a wall to receive putlogs, the horizontal timbers which support scaffolding boards; sometimes not filled after construction is complete. Also called putholes or putlock holes.

**PUTTO** (plural: putti)   Painting or carving of a small naked boy.

**QUADRIPARTITE RIB-VAULT**  A *vault* with two pairs of *diagonal ribs* dividing each *bay* into four triangular compartments or *cells* [37].

**QUARRIES**  Square (or diamond) panes of glass supported by lead strips (*cames*); square floor slabs or tiles.

**QUATREFOIL**  A four-lobed opening [4, 34].

**QUATTROCENTO**  The Italian *Renaissance* architecture of the 15th century; also used for its 19th-century revival.

**QUEEN ANNE**  Not to be confused with the architecture of the reign of Queen Anne (1702–14), this usually refers to a later Victorian style that sought to revive the domestic *classical* manner of the mid 17th century. It favoured red brick or *terracotta*, usually combined with white-painted woodwork. It is particularly associated with the architect Richard Norman Shaw (1831–1912) and with the turn away from the *Gothic Revival* [pl. 48].

**QUEENPOSTS**  Paired vertical or near-vertical timbers placed symmetrically on a *tie-beam* of a roof to support *purlins* (horizontal longitudinal timbers).

**QUEEN-STRUTS**  Paired vertical or near-vertical timbers placed symmetrically on a *tie-beam* of a roof to support the *rafters*, and not directly attached to the longitudinal timbers [34].

**QUIRK**  Sharp groove to one side of a convex medieval *moulding*.

**QUOINS** Dressed or otherwise emphasized stones at the angles of a building, or their imitation in brick or other materials [29].

**RADBURN SYSTEM** Vehicle and pedestrian segregation in residential developments, based on that used at Radburn, New Jersey, USA, by Wright and Stein, 1928–30.

**RADIATING CHAPELS** Chapels projecting radially from an *ambulatory* or *apse*, usually at the east end of a large church.

**RAFTERS** Inclined lateral timbers supporting the roof covering. **COMMON RAFTERS**: regularly spaced uniform rafters placed along the length of a roof or between *principals*; also called **COUPLED RAFTERS**. **PRINCIPAL RAFTERS**: rafters which also act as principals, i.e. the paired inclined lateral timbers of a *truss* [34].

**RAGGLE** Groove cut in masonry, especially to receive the edge of a roof-covering.

**RAGULY** Ragged (in heraldry). Also applied to funerary sculpture, e.g. **CROSS RAGULY**: with a notched outline.

**RAIL** A horizontal member in *panelling* or in a timber-framed wall [24, 34]. See also *edge rail*, *plate rail* (railways).

**RAINWATER-HEAD** A container at the top of a downpipe, usually of lead, into which rainwater runs from the gutters.

**RAISED AND FIELDED** Of *panelling*, with the central area of the panel (*field*) raised up [24]. Also used for stonework treated with sunk or raised panels.

**RAKED** Sloped or pitched.

**RAMPART** Defensive outer wall of stone or earth.
**RAMPART WALK**: path along the inner face.

**RAMPED** Of a stair-rail, *dado* etc: with a steep concave curve just short of the *newel*, or in line with it.

**RANDOM RUBBLE** See *rubble*.

**RATCOURSE** (Scots): Projecting *string course* on a *doocot* (dovecote) to deter rats.

**RATH** (Irish): Circular or near-circular enclosure consisting of one or more earthen (or occasionally stone) banks, classified according to the number of surrounding ditches as *univallate*, *bivallate* or *trivallate*. Most date from early Christian times and housed single farms or served as cattle enclosures for farms. Also called *ring forts*.

**REBATE** Rectangular section cut out of a masonry edge to receive a shutter, door, window, etc.

**REBUS** A heraldic pun, e.g. a fiery cock for Cockburn.

**REEDING** Series of convex *mouldings*, the reverse of *fluting*.

**REFECTORY** Dining hall of a monastery, college or similar establishment.

**REGENCY** Used generally for the late *Georgian* architecture of *c.* 1800–30, which favoured thinner or more summary *classical* detail than the 18th-century norm [pls 44, 45]. (Vogue Regency refers to its revival as a fashionable style of the 1920s–50s.)

**REINFORCED** Of *concrete*: incorporating steel rods to take the tensile force.

**RELIEVING ARCH** An *arch* incorporated in a wall to relieve superimposed weight [3]. Also called a *discharging arch*.

**RENAISSANCE** The revival of *classical* architecture that began in 15th-century Italy and spread through Western Europe and the Americas in the following two centuries, finding distinctive forms and interpretations in different states and regions. From *c.* 1830 the Italian version was revived in Britain as a style in its own right (sometimes called *Neo-Renaissance* or *Italianate*), i.e. as distinguished from the native *Georgian* classical tradition.

**RENDERING** The covering of outside walls with a uniform mortar or plaster surface or skin for protection from the weather. **CEMENT RENDERING**: a cheaper substitute for *stucco* (fine lime plaster), usually with a grainy texture.

**REPOUSSÉ**  Relief designs in metalwork, formed by beating it from the back.

**RERE-ARCH**  Archway in medieval architecture formed across the wide inner opening of a window.

**REREDORTER**  (*lit.* behind the dormitory): Latrines in a monastery or abbey, usually placed east of the *cloister*.

**REREDOS**  Painted and/or sculpted *screen* behind and above an altar.

**RESPOND**  Half-pier or *half-column* bonded into a wall and carrying one end of an *arch*. It usually terminates an *arcade*. A *pilaster* respond is set at the end of a *colonnade*, arcade etc. to balance visually the *column* which it faces.

**RETABLE**  Painted or carved panel standing on or at the back of an altar, usually attached to it.

**RETICULATED TRACERY**  A form of *bar tracery* used in the early 14th century, with net-like patterns of *ogee*- (double-curved) ended lozenges [4].

**RETROCHOIR**  In a major church, the area behind the high altar and east chapel.

**RETURN**  Part of a wall or *moulding* that continues at a different angle, usually a right-angle.

**REVEAL**  The plane of a *jamb*, between the wall and the frame of a door or window.

**RHONE**  (Scots): Gutter along the *eaves* for rainwater.

**RIBBON POINTING**  Mortar joints formed with a trowel so that they stand out.

**RIBBONWORK**  Ornament in the form of long trailing ribbons, common in Elizabethan and Jacobean times.

**RIB-VAULT**  A *vault* with a masonry framework of intersecting *arches* (ribs) supporting *cells*, used in *Gothic* and late *Norman* architecture [37]. A *wall-rib* or wall arch spans between wall and cell vault. A *transverse rib* spans between two walls to divide a vault into *bays*. In a *quadripartite rib-vault*, each bay has two pairs of *diagonal ribs* dividing the vault into four triangular cells. A *sexpartite rib-vault*, usually set over paired bays, has an extra pair of ribs *springing* from between the bays. More elaborate vaults may include ridge-ribs along the *crown* of a vault or bisecting the bays; *tiercerons*, extra decorative ribs springing from the corners of a bay; and *liernes*, short decorative ribs in the crown of a vault, not linked to any springing point. A *stellar* or *star-vault* has liernes in star formation. A *fan-vault* is a form of vault used after *c.* 1350, made up of halved concave masonry cones decorated with *blind tracery*.

**RIDGE OR RIDGE-PIECE** Horizontal longitudinal timber at the apex of a roof, supporting the ends of the *rafters* [34, 37].

**RINCEAU** (*lit.* little branch): *Classical* ornament of leafy scrolls branching alternately to left and right [28].

Fig. 28 Rinceau

**RING CRYPT** A corridor *crypt* surrounding the *apse* of an early medieval church, often associated with chambers for relics.

**RING FORT** (Irish): Circular or near-circular enclosure consisting of one or more earthen (or occasionally stone) banks, classified according to the number of surrounding ditches as *univallate*, *bivallate* or *trivallate*. Most date from early Christian times and housed single farms or served as cattle enclosures for farms. Also called a *rath*.

**RINGING CHAMBER** Stage in a tower where the bell ringers stand.

**RISER** Vertical face of a step [32].

**ROACH** A rough-textured form of *Portland stone*, with small cavities and fossil shells.

**ROCAILLE** (French): Asymmetrical arrangements of unworked rocks, or its imitation in other materials, associated especially with the *Rococo* style; also called *rockwork*.

**ROCK-FACED** Masonry cleft to produce a natural, rugged appearance.

**ROCKWORK**  Asymmetrical arrangements of unworked rocks, or its imitation in other materials, associated especially with the *Rococo* style; also called *rocaille*.

**ROCOCO**  A style of 18th-century decoration characterized by asymmetrical ornament, often in C- or S-shapes usually derived from foliage or shells. It began in France, flourishing most fully there and in Germany and Central Europe. It is sometimes associated with the imitation Chinese manner known as *Chinoiserie*, and, in the British Isles, with the phase of the *Gothic Revival* known as *Gothick* [pl. 42].

**ROLL MOULDING**  Medieval *moulding* of semicircular or more than semi-circular section [21].

**ROMAN**  The architecture of the Roman Empire, to which most of Britain belonged from 43 to *c.* 410 A.D. Our knowledge of Romano-British architecture depends mostly on *archaeological* reconstructions from foundations and fragments, though some notable fortifications and other military works survive above ground level in recognizable form.

**ROMAN DORIC**  A common version of the simplest and plainest of the three main *classical orders*, which features a *frieze* with *triglyphs* and *metopes*. A Roman Doric *column* has a simple round *capital* with a narrow neck band and a plain or fluted *shaft*, resting on a circular base [23]. Compare *Greek Doric*.

**ROMANESQUE**  The dominant style of Western Europe in the 11th and 12th centuries. It is associated especially with the expansion of monasticism and the building of large stone churches, and is characterized by massive masonry, round-headed *arches* and *vaulting* inspired by ancient *Roman* precedent, and by the use of stylized ornament. In England it is commonly known as *Norman*.

**ROOD**  Crucifix flanked by the Virgin and St John, usually over the entry into the *chancel*, set on a beam (rood beam) or painted on the wall. The rood *screen* below often had a walkway along the top, reached by a rood stair in the side wall.

**ROPE MOULDING**  A *moulding* like twisted strands of a rope; also called *cable moulding*.

**ROSE WINDOW**   Circular window with *tracery* radiating from the centre.

**ROSETTE**   A flat circular ornament in the shape of a flower.

**ROTUNDA**   Building or room circular in plan.

**ROUGHCAST**   External wall plaster mixed with a coarse *aggregate* such as gravel and applied by throwing with the motion of a backhand stroke in tennis.

**ROUND**   (Scots): A rounded *bartizan* or turret, usually roofless. An *angle round* is set at a corner.

**ROVING BRIDGE**   (canals): A bridge carrying a towing path from one bank to the other, arranged with reverse curves so that horses towing boats did not need to be unhitched.

**RUBBED BRICKWORK**   Soft brick sawn roughly, then rubbed to a precise (gauged) surface. Mostly used for door or window openings. Also called *gauged brickwork*.

**RUBBLE**   Masonry whose stones are wholly or partly in a rough state. **COURSED**: *coursed* stones with rough faces. **RANDOM**: uncoursed stones in a random pattern. **SNECKED**: with courses broken by smaller stones (snecks).

**RUNDBOGENSTIL**   (German, *lit.* round-arched style): A simplified style developed in early 19th-century Germany, drawing on *Early Christian*, *Byzantine*, *Romanesque* and early *Renaissance* precedents; sometimes echoed in British 19th-century buildings.

**RUSTICATION**   Exaggerated treatment of masonry to give an effect of strength. The joints are usually recessed, by V-section *chamfering* or square-section channelling (*channelled rustication*) [29]. **BANDED RUSTICATION** has only the horizontal joints emphasized. The faces may be flat, but can be *diamond-faced*, like shallow pyramids, *vermiculated*, with a stylized texture like worm-casts, and glacial, like icicles or stalactites (also called *frost-work*). Rusticated *columns* may have their *shafts* treated in any of these ways.

**RYBATS**   (Scots): Dressed stones at the edges of an opening. Also called *margins*.

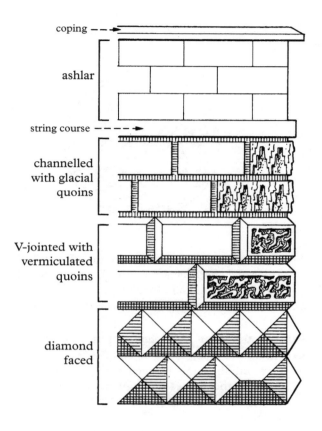

Fig. 29   Rustication

**SACRAMENT HOUSE**  Safe cupboard in a side wall of the *chancel* of a church and not directly associated with an altar, for reservation of the sacrament.

**SACRISTY**  Room in a church for sacred vessels and vestments.

**SADDLEBACK ROOF**  A pitched roof used on a tower [7].

**SAIL DOME**  A square dome or *vault* of one continuous curve with the same diameter as the diagonal of the square, so that it rises from *pendentives* between *arches*. So named from its supposed resemblance to a billowing sail. Also called a *sail vault*.

**SAIL VAULT**  A square *vault* or dome of one continuous curve with the same diameter as the diagonal of the square, so that it rises from *pendentives* between *arches*. So named from its supposed resemblance to a billowing sail. Also called a *sail dome*.

**SALOMONIC COLUMNS**  *Columns* with twisted spiral *shafts*, called after columns in Rome supposed to have come from Solomon's Temple in Jerusalem. Also called *Solomonic columns, barley-sugar columns*.

**SALTIRE CROSS**  A cross with arms set diagonally.

**SANCTUARY**  The area around the main altar of a church.

**SANGHA**  Residence of Buddhist monks or nuns.

**SARCOPHAGUS**  (*lit.* flesh-consuming): Coffin of stone or other durable material.

**SARKING** (Scots): Boards laid on the *rafters* to support the roof covering.

**SASH WINDOW** A window with a glazed section or section that opens by sliding in grooves.

**SAUCER DOME** An internal dome of flattened profile.

**SAXO-NORMAN** *Transitional Romanesque* style combining *Anglo-Saxon* and *Norman* features, current *c.* 1060–1100.

**SCAGLIOLA** Polished composition covering giving the effect of (usually coloured) marble, used especially on *columns* from the mid-18th to early 19th century.

**SCALE-AND-PLATT STAIR** (Scots; *lit.* stair and landing): with parallel flights rising alternately in opposite directions, without an open well.

**SCALLOPED CAPITAL** A form of *block capital* in which the convex lower faces are carved with broad *flutings* or half-cones [21].

**SCARCEMENT** Extra thickness of the lower part of a wall, e.g. to carry a floor.

**SCARP** Artificial cutting away of the ground to form a steep slope.

**SCISSOR TRUSS** A roof *truss* framed at the bottom by crossed intersecting beams like open scissors [34].

**SCISSOR-BRACES** In a timber roof, paired *braces* crossing diagonally between pairs of *rafters* or *principals* [34].

**SCOTIA** A hollow *classical moulding*, especially on a *column base* [23].

**SCOTTISH OR SCOTCH BARONIAL** A Victorian style based on the fortified and semi-fortified Scottish houses of the 16th and 17th centuries. The distinguishing features are vertical rather than horizontal emphasis, small windows, steep roofs, small turrets or *tourelles*, and a sparing use of *Renaissance* ornament [pl. 50].

**SCREEN** In a medieval church, usually set at the entry to the *chancel*. A *parclose screen* separates a chapel from the rest of the church. A *rood* screen was placed below a representation of the Crucifixion (called a rood).

**SCREENS PASSAGE** In an older house or college, a screened-off entrance passage between great hall and service rooms.

**SCRIBE** (Scots): To cut and mark timber against an irregular stone or plaster surface.

**SCUNTION** (Scots): A *reveal*, i.e. the plane of a *jamb* between the wall and the frame of a door or window.

**SECTION** Two-dimensional representation of a building, *moulding* etc., revealed by cutting across it.

**SEDILIA** (singular: sedile) Seats for the priests (usually three) in the wall on the south side of the *chancel* of a church or chapel.

**SEGMENTAL PEDIMENT** A *pediment* with a segmental (part-circular) top [25].

**SEPTUM** Low wall between the *choir* and *nave* of a church.

**SERLIAN WINDOW** In *classical* architecture, a window with an arched central *light* flanked by two lower straight-headed ones; the motif is also used for other openings. Also called a Serlian motif, Serliana, *Palladian window* and *Venetian window*.

**SESSION HOUSE** (Scots): A room or separate building for meetings of the elders who form a kirk session, or a shelter by the entrance to a church or churchyard for an elder collecting for poor relief; built at the expense of a kirk session. A sessions house is an English term for a court house.

**SET-BACK BUTTRESS** A *buttress* placed slightly back from the angle of a building [7].

**SET-OFF** Inclined, projecting surface to keep water away from the wall below. Also called *weathering*.

**SETTS** Squared stones, usually of granite, used for paving or flooring.

**SEXFOIL** A six-lobed opening.

**SEXPARTITE RIB-VAULT** A *rib-vault*, usually set over paired *bays*, with an extra pair of ribs *springing* from between the bays.

**SGRAFFITO** (Italian): Decoration scratched, often in plaster, to reveal a pattern in another colour beneath.

**SHAFT** Vertical member of round or polygonal section, including the main part of a *classical column*, and by extension also of a *pilaster* [21, 23].

**SHAFT-RING** A ring around a circular *pier* or a *shaft* attached to a pier, typical of the 12th and 13th centuries [13]. Also called an *annulet*.

**SHAPED GABLE** A *gable* with curved sides [14].

**SHEILA-NA-GIG** Female fertility figure, usually with legs apart.

**SHELL** Thin, self-supporting roofing membrane of timber or *concrete*.

**SHEUGH** (Scots): A trench or open drain; a street gutter.

**SHINGLES** Thin pieces of wood like overlapping tiles, used externally.

**SHOULDERED ARCH** An *arch* with arcs in each corner and a flat centre or *lintel* [3].

**SHOULDERED ARCHITRAVE** The moulded frame of a door or window with horizontal and vertical projections at the top angles [30].

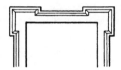

Fig. 30   Shouldered architrave

**SHUTTERING** Temporary framing of timber, metal, plastic, etc used for casting *concrete*; also called *formwork*.

**SIDE PURLINS** Pairs of longitudinal timbers placed some way up the slope of the roof, which carry *common rafters*.

**SILL** Horizontal member at the bottom of a window or door frame; sometimes spelt cill. Also the horizontal member at the *base* of a timber-framed wall, into which the *posts* and *studs* are tenoned [34].

**SINGLE-FRAMED** Of a roof: without *purlins* or other longitudinal members above the *springing* of the *rafters*. Compare *double-framed*.

**SKEW** (Scots): Sloping or shaped stones finishing a *gable* upstanding from the roof. A skewputt is a *bracket* at the bottom end of a skew.

**SKEW ARCH** An *arch* spanning *responds* not diametrically opposed; hence also skew bridge.

**SLAB BLOCK**  A *multi-storey* block with flats approached from corridors or galleries from service cores at intervals or towers at the ends (plan also used for offices, hotels etc.).

**SLATE-HANGING**  Covering of overlapping slates on a wall, which is then said to be slate-hung. *Tile-hanging* is similar.

**SLOP STONE**  (Irish): Drainage stone designed to carry kitchen waste through the thickness of a wall.

**SLYPE**  In a greater medieval church, a covered way or passage leading east from the *cloisters* between *transept* and *chapter house*.

**SNECKED**  Of masonry, with *courses* broken by smaller stones (snecks).

**SOFFIT**  (*lit.* ceiling): Underside of an *arch* (also called an *intrados*), *lintel*, etc. **SOFFIT ROLL**: medieval *roll moulding* on a soffit.

**SOLAR**  Private upper chamber in a medieval house, accessible from the high or *dais* end of the great hall.

**SOLOMONIC COLUMNS**  *Columns* with twisted spiral *shafts*, called after columns in Rome supposed to have come from Solomon's Temple in Jerusalem. Also called *Salomonic columns, barley-sugar columns*.

**SOPRAPORTA**  Painting or relief above an internal door. Also called an *overdoor*.

**SOUNDING-BOARD**  Flat canopy over a pulpit to reflect the preacher's voice downwards to the congregation; also called a *tester*.

**SOUTERRAIN**  Underground stone-lined passage and chamber.

**SPACE FRAME**  A three-dimensional framework in which all the members are interconnected, designed to cover very large areas.

**SPANDRELS**  Roughly triangular spaces between an *arch* and its containing rectangle, or between adjacent arches [3]. Also non-structural panels under the windows, especially on a curtain-walled building.

**SPERE**  A fixed structure screening the lower end of the great hall from the *screens passage*. **SPERE TRUSS**: roof *truss* incorporated in the spere.

**SPIKE**  A thin *spire* of timber and lead, rising from the centre of a tower roof.

**SPIRAL STAIR**  A stair in a circular well with a central supporting *newel*. Also called a *vice* or (Scots) turnpike stair.

**SPIRE**  Tall pyramidal or conical feature crowning a tower or turret [7]. **BROACH**: starting from a square *base*, then carried into an octagonal section by means of triangular faces. **SPLAYED-FOOT**: variation of the broach form, found in England principally in the south-east, in which the four cardinal faces are splayed out near their bases, to cover the corners, while oblique (or intermediate) faces taper away to a point. **NEEDLE SPIRE**: thin spire rising from the centre of a tower roof, well inside the *parapet*.

**SPIRELET**  Slender *spire* on the *ridge* of a roof. Also called a *flèche*.

**SPLAT**  A flat board with shaped sides, especially a *baluster* (called a splat baluster).

**SPLAYED**  Of an opening: wider on one face of the wall than the other.

**SPLAYED-FOOT SPIRE**  A variant of the *broach spire*, found in England principally in the south-east, in which the four cardinal faces are splayed out near their *bases*, to cover the corners, while oblique (or intermediate) faces taper away to a point [7].

**SPLIT CUSP**  In *tracery* in the *Gothic* style, a cusp or curved projection which has a v-shaped opening set within the apex. Also called a *Kentish cusp*.

**SPRING OR SPRINGING**  Level at which at *arch* or *vault* rises from its supports [37]. **SPRINGERS**: the lowest stones of an arch or vaulting rib.

**SPROCKET**  In a roof, a short timber placed on the back and at the foot of a rafter to form projecting *eaves* [34]; hence a sprocketed roof.

**SPUR**  Diagonal projection at the *base* of a *moulding*, *column*, or *buttress* (called a spur buttress).

**SQUARE PANEL**  A form of timber-framed wall in which the main uprights (*posts*) and horizontals (*rails*) form large square or near-square compartments [34]. Compare *close studding*.

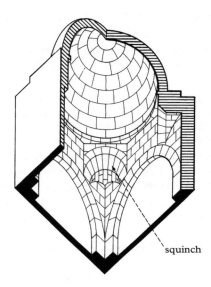

squinch

Fig. 31   Squinch (in a dome)

**SQUINCH**   *Arch* or series of arches thrown across an interior angle of a square or rectangular structure to support a circular or polygonal superstructure, especially a dome or *spire* [31].

**SQUINT**   An aperture in a wall or through a *pier*, usually to allow a view of an altar. Also called a *hagioscope*.

**STACK**   A chimneystack.

**STACK BOND**   Non-structural brick facing, using bricks laid long side outwards and in vertical (i.e. non-overlapping) tiers.

**STALL**   Fixed seat in the *choir* or *chancel* of a church for the clergy or choir. Usually with armrests, and often framed together.

**STANCHION**   Upright structural member, of iron, steel or *reinforced concrete*.

**STANDPIPE TOWER**   Containing a *column* of water to regulate pressure in water mains. Also called a *manometer tower*.

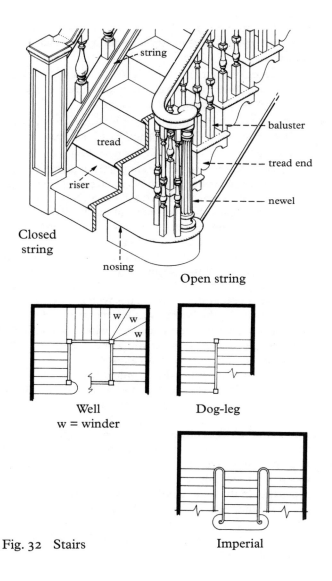

string

tread

riser

Closed
string

nosing

baluster

tread end

newel

Open string

Well
w = winder

Dog-leg

Imperial

Fig. 32    Stairs

**STAR-VAULT** With *liernes* (short decorative ribs not linked to any *springing* point) in star formation. Also called a *stellar vault*.

**STAY-SUSPENSION BRIDGE** A *suspension bridge* supported by diagonal stays from towers or pylons direct to the deck; also called a cable-stayed bridge.

**STEADING** (Scots): Farm building or buildings, most often the principal group of agricultural buildings on a farm.

**STEAM ENGINES** All early examples were house engines in which a masonry structure supported a pivoted beam, hence the generic term beam engine. Their prime use was for pumping. In 1711/12 Thomas Newcomen (1663-1729) made the first practical machines, which worked on the atmospheric principle, condensing steam to create a vacuum under a piston which was then forced downwards by the pressure of the atmosphere on its upper surface, thus rocking the overhead beam to which the piston was fastened. A lift pump was attached at the other end of the beam. James Watt's developments of the Newcomen engine included a separate condenser (patented 1769), which saved much fuel, though his early engines still worked on the atmospheric principle. Watt's zealous defence of his patents thwarted further development for several decades, but later types included rotative engines which drove a flywheel. Richard Trevithick (1771–1823) pioneered the high pressure engine which, in the beam configuration, was known as the Cornish engine, after his birthplace and the area of its finest manufacturers. High pressure engines could be simple, in which the steam was used only once, or compound where, after expansion in the first cylinder, exhaust steam was fed into a second, larger cylinder, where it did more useful work before venting to atmosphere. Triple, or even quadruple, expansion came later for high-speed mill engines driving factory machinery.

**STEEPLE** Tower together with a *spire*, *lantern*, or *belfry*.

**STELLAR VAULT** With *liernes* (short decorative ribs not linked to any *springing* point) in star formation. Also called a *star-vault*.

**STIFF-LEAF** English type of late 12th- and early 13th-century decoration in the form of thick uncurling foliage [33].

Fig. 33   Stiff-leaf capital

**STILTED ARCH**   With a vertical section above the *impost*, i.e. the horizontal *moulding* at the *springing* [3].

**STOCK BRICKS**   The better kind of bricks, used for outward facing; compare *place bricks*. Also the yellowish kind of bricks much used in and around London.

**STOP**   Plain or decorated terminal to *mouldings* or *chamfers* at the end of *hoodmoulds* and *labels* (*label stop*), or *string courses*. A *headstop* is carved with a head.

**STOUP**   Vessel for holy water, usually near a door.

**STRAINER ARCH**   An *arch* inserted in an opening to resist inward pressure.

**STRAPWORK**   Late 16th and early 17th-century decoration, like interlaced leather straps.

**STRETCHER**   A brick laid with its long side outermost [6].

**STRETCHER BOND**   Brickwork with only the *stretchers* (long sides) of the bricks showing.

**STRING**   A sloping member holding the ends of the *treads* and *risers* of a staircase [32]. A **CLOSED STRING** has a continuous upper edge and covers the ends of the treads and risers. An **OPEN STRING** is cut into the shape of the treads and risers.

**STRING COURSE**   Horizontal *course* or *moulding* projecting from the surface of a wall [29].

**STRUT**   Vertical or oblique timber between two members of a *truss*, not directly supporting longitudinal timbers. On a *tie-beam*, *queen-struts* are in pairs, a *king-strut* is placed centrally; compare *queenposts*, *kingpost*.

**STUCCO**   A durable lime plaster, sometimes incorporating marble dust. It can be shaped into ornamental or architectural features, or used externally as a protective coating.

**STUDS** Subsidiary vertical timbers of a timber-framed wall or partition. *Close studding* has closely set studs of equal size [34].

**STUGGED** (Scots): Of masonry, hacked or picked as a key for *rendering*; used as a surface finish in the 19th century.

**STUPA** Buddhist shrine, circular in plan.

**STYLOBATE** Top of the solid platform on which a *classical colonnade* stands [23].

**SUB-CUSPING** Cusping (projecting points formed by curves, especially within the *tracery* of *Gothic* architecture) in which the sides of the *cusps* have smaller cusps in turn.

**SUNK CHAMFER** A deeply recessed surface, formed by cutting into a square edge or corner [8].

**SUPERIMPOSED ORDERS** *Classical orders* on successive levels, customarily in the upward sequence of *Tuscan, Doric, Ionic, Corinthian, Composite.*

**SUSPENSION BRIDGE** A bridge with the roadway or deck suspended from cables or chains slung between towers or pylons.

**SWAG** Ornament in the form of drapery suspended from both ends. Compare *festoon.*

**SWAN-NECK PEDIMENT** A *broken pediment* with double-curved sides [25].

**SYSTEM BUILDING** System of manufactured units assembled on site. Also called industrial building.

**TABERNACLE** Canopied structure in a church or chapel to contain the reserved sacrament or a relic. Also an architectural frame for an image or statue.

**TABLE TOMB** Memorial slab raised on free-standing legs.

**TAS-DE-CHARGE** (French): The lower *courses* of a *vault* or *arch* which are laid horizontally [37].

**TEMPIETTO** (Italian, little temple): A small temple-like building, usually round and domed.

**TEMPLE FRONT** The front features of a *portico* applied to a wall; also called a *blind portico*.

**TENEMENT** (Scots): A purpose-built *flatted* block.

**TENONED PURLINS** *Purlins* (horizontal longitudinal timbers in a roof structure) tenoned into either side of the *principals*. Also called *butt purlins*.

**TERM** *Pedestal* or *pilaster* tapering downward, usually with the upper part of a human figure growing out of it; sometimes called a terminal figure.

**TERQUETRA** A symbolic figure in the form of a three-cornered knot of interlaced arcs, common in Celtic art. Also called *triquetra*.

**TERRACOTTA** Moulded and fired clay ornament or *cladding*; when glazed and coloured or left white often called *faience*.

**TERREPLEIN** (French, *lit.* earth-filled): In a fort, the level surface of a *rampart* behind a *parapet* for mounting guns.

**TESSELLATED PAVEMENT**  Mosaic flooring, particularly Roman, made of tesserae, i.e. small cubes of glass, stone or brick.

**TESTER**  (*lit.* head): Flat canopy over a tomb or *pulpit*, where it is also called a *sounding-board*.

**TESTER TOMB**  *Tomb-chest* with effigies beneath a flat canopy (*tester*), either free-standing (tester with four or more *columns*), or attached to a wall (*half-tester*) with columns on one side only.

**TETRASTYLE**  Of a porch or *portico*: with four *columns* across the front.

**THERMAL WINDOW**  A semicircular window with two *mullions*; also called a *Diocletian window* after its use in the Baths of Diocletian, Rome.

**THOLSEL**  (Irish): An exchange or market house; the English term is *tolsey*.

**THREE-CENTRED ARCH**  An *arch* with a rounded top, but curving inward more at the sides [3]; also called a *depressed arch*.

**THREE-DECKER PULPIT**  A raised and enclosed platform for the preaching of sermons, with a reading desk below and clerk's desk below that. Compare *two-decker pulpit*.

**THROUGH PURLINS**  *Purlins* (horizontal longitudinal timbers in a roof structure) which pass through or past the *principals*; they include *clasped purlins*, which rest on *queenposts* or are carried in the angle between principals and *collar*, and *trenched purlins* which are trenched into the backs of the principals.

**TIDAL GATES**  (Canals): Single pair of gates allowing vessels to pass when the tide makes a level.

**TIE-BEAM**  Main horizontal transverse timber in a roof structure, which carries the feet of the *principals* at wall level [34].

**TIERCERON**  In a *rib-vault*, an extra decorative rib *springing* from the corner of a *bay* [37]; hence tierceron vault.

**TIFTING**  (Scots): a mortar bed for verge slates laid over the *gable skew*.

**TILE-HANGING**  Covering of overlapping tiles on a wall, which is then said to be tile-hung. *Slate-hanging* is similar.

**TILTYARD**  An open area used for jousting.

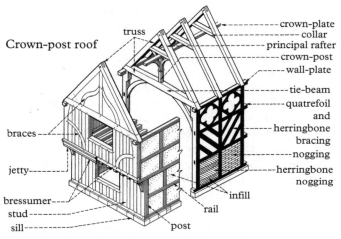

Crown-post roof

truss

crown-plate
collar
principal rafter
crown-post
wall-plate
tie-beam
quatrefoil
and
herringbone
bracing
nogging
herringbone
nogging

braces

jetty

bressumer
stud
sill

infill

rail

post

Box frame:  i) Close studding   ii) Square panel

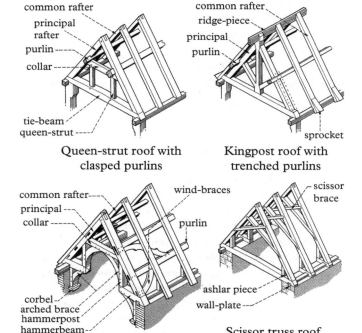

common rafter
principal
rafter
purlin
collar

tie-beam
queen-strut

Queen-strut roof with
clasped purlins

common rafter
ridge-piece
principal
purlin

sprocket

Kingpost roof with
trenched purlins

common rafter
principal
collar

wind-braces

purlin

corbel
arched brace
hammerpost
hammerbeam

Hammerbeam roof with
butt purlins

scissor
brace

ashlar piece
wall-plate

Scissor truss roof

Fig. 34  Timber framing

125

**TIMBER FRAMING**   Method of construction in which the structural frame is built of interlocking timbers [34]. In *close studding* the uprights (*studs*) are set close together, in *square panel* construction the main uprights (*posts*) and horizontals (*rails*) form large square or near-square compartments. The spaces are filled with non-structural material, e.g. *infill* of wattle and daub, lath and plaster, brickwork (known as *nogging*), etc. and may be covered by plaster, *weatherboarding* (overlapping horizontal boards), or tiles [pls 25, 39].

**TOLBOOTH**   (Scots; *lit.* tax booth): Tax office containing burgh council chamber and prison.

**TOLSEY**   An exchange or market house; the Irish term is *tholsel*.

**TOMB-CHEST**   Chest-shaped tomb, usually of stone.

**TONDO**   A circular painting or relief.

**TORUS** (plural: tori)   Large convex *moulding* usually used on a *classical column base* [23].

**TOUCH**   Soft black marble quarried near Tournai in Belgium.

**TOURELLE**   Turret *corbelled* out from the wall [35].

**TOWER ARCH**   *Arch* joining a church tower to the *nave*.

**TOWER BLOCK**   A generic term for any very high *multi-storey* building.

**TOWER HOUSE**   (Scots and Irish): Compact fortified house with the main hall raised above the ground and at least one more storey above it [35]. The type continued well into the 17th century in its modified forms: **L-PLAN**, with a *jamb* or wing at one corner; **Z-PLAN**, with a jamb or wing at each diagonally opposite corner.

**TRABEATED**   Dependent structurally on the upright (*post*) and beam (*lintel*) principle. Compare *arcuated*.

**TRACERY**   Openwork pattern of masonry or timber in an opening, especially the upper part of an opening; most common in *Gothic* architecture. **BLIND TRACERY** is applied to a solid wall. **PLATE TRACERY**, the earliest form, introduced *c.* 1200, has shapes cut through solid masonry [26]. **BAR TRACERY**, introduced *c.* 1250, has patterns are formed by intersecting moulded ribwork continuing upwards from the *mullions* [4]. *Bar tracery* types include: **CURVILINEAR TRACERY**, with uninterrupted flowing

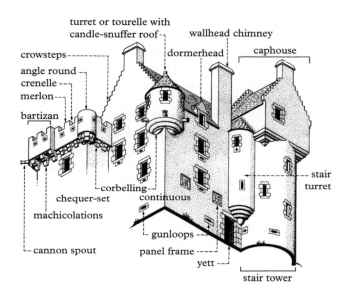

Fig. 35   The Tower House: elements

curves, typical of the 14th century (also called **FLOWING TRACERY**); **GEOMETRICAL TRACERY**, typical of *c.* 1250–*c.* 1310, which uses simple forms, especially circles; **INTERSECTING TRACERY**, used *c.* 1300, formed by interlocking mullions each branching out in two curved bars of the same radius but different centres; **LOOP TRACERY** (Scots), used *c.* 1500–45, with large uncusped loop-like forms; **PANEL TRACERY**, with even upright divisions made by a horizontal *transom* or transoms; **RETICULATED TRACERY**, early 14th century, with net-like patterns of *ogee-* (double-curved) ended lozenges; **Y-TRACERY**, used *c.* 1300, which branches into a Y-shape.

**TRADES LOFT**   (Scots): A *gallery* in a church reserved for a special group. Compare *laird's loft*.

**TRANSE**   (Scots): A passage, especially a *screens passage*, i.e. a screened-off entrance passage between great hall and service rooms in an older house or college.

**TRANSEPT**   Transverse portion of a church.

**TRANSEPTAL CHAPEL**   A chapel in the position of a *transept* and opening to the *nave* through a single *arch*, but without a full central *crossing*.

**TRANSITIONAL**   Generally used for the period *c.* 1175–*c.* 1200, between *Norman* and the first (*Early English*) period of *Gothic*, in which details of the later style are often used on the general forms of the earlier [pl. 4].

**TRANSOM**   Horizontal member separating window *lights* [4].

**TRANSVERSE ARCH**   An *arch* spanning a main axis (e.g. of a *vaulted* space).

**TRANSVERSE RIB**   A rib spanning between two walls to divide a *rib-vault* into *bays* [37].

**TREAD**   Horizontal part of a step. The tread end may be carved on a staircase [32].

**TREFOIL**   A three-lobed opening [4].

**TRENCHED PURLINS**   *Purlins* (horizontal longitudinal timbers in a roof structure) which are trenched into the backs of the *principals* [34].

**TRIFORIUM**   Middle storey of a church interior treated as an *arcaded* wall passage or *blind arcade*, its height corresponding to that of the *aisle* roof.

**TRIGLYPHS**   (*lit.* three-grooved tablets): Stylized beam-ends in a *Doric frieze*, with *metopes* between [23].

**TRIQUETRA**   A symbolic figure in the form of a three-cornered knot of interlaced arcs, common in Celtic art. Compare *terquetra*.

**TRIUMPHAL ARCH**   Influential type of Roman Imperial monument, free-standing, with a square *attic* or top section and broad sections to either side of the main opening, often with lesser openings or *columns*.

**TRIVALLATE**   Of a *hill-fort*: defended by three concentric banks and ditches.

**TROMPE L'OEIL**   (French, *lit.* trick the eye): Two-dimensional painting or decoration in which objects are represented three-dimensionally.

**TROPHY**   Sculpted or painted group of arms or armour.

**TRUMEAU**   (French): Central stone upright supporting the *tympanum* of a wide doorway, especially of a medieval church. **TRUMEAU FIGURE**: carved figure attached to it; compare *column figure*.

**TRUMPET CAPITAL**  *Capital* with concave lower part, usually *scalloped*, in use in the later 12th century [36].

Fig. 36  Trumpet capital

**TRUSS**  *Braced* framework, spanning between supports [34]. Types include: **BELFAST ROOF TRUSS**: a wide segmental truss built as a lattice-beam, originally using short cuts of timber left over from shipbuilding in Belfast; **CLOSED TRUSS** (of a roof): with the spaces between the timbers filled, to form an internal partition or partitions; **SPERE TRUSS**: roof truss incorporated in a *spere* (a fixed structure screening the lower end of a great hall from the *screens passage* in an older house, college, etc.)

**TUCK POINTING**  Exposed mortar jointing of masonry or brickwork with a narrow central channel filled with finer, whiter mortar.

**TUDOR**  Strictly, the architecture of the English Tudor dynasty (1485–1603), but used more often for late *Gothic* secular buildings especially of the first half of the 16th century. These use a simplified version of *Perpendicular*, characterised by straight-headed *mullioned* windows with arched *lights*, and by rooflines with steep *gables* and tall chimneys, often asymmetrically placed [pls 10, 12, 13, 26].

**TUDOR ARCH**  An *arch* with arcs in each corner joining straight lines to the central point [3].

**TUMBLING OR TUMBLING-IN**  *Courses* of brickwork laid at right-angles to a slope, e.g. of a *gable*, forming triangles by tapering into horizontal courses [14].

**TUNNEL VAULT**  The simplest kind of *vault*, in the form of a continuous semicircular or pointed *arch*; also called a *barrel vault*.

**TUSCAN**   One of the *orders* of *classical* architecture, a
simpler variant of *Roman Doric* [23].

**TUSKING STONES**   (Scots): Projecting end stones for
bonding with an adjoining wall.

**TWO-CENTRED ARCH**   The simplest kind of pointed *arch*
[3].

**TWO-DECKER PULPIT**   A raised and enclosed platform for
the preaching of sermons, with a reading desk below.
Compare *three-decker pulpit*.

**TYMPANUM**   The surface between a *lintel* and the *arch*
above it, or within a *pediment* [27].

**UNDERCROFT** Usually describes the *vaulted* room or rooms beneath the main room or rooms of a medieval house. Compare *crypt*.

**UNDERSHOT WATER WHEEL** One turned by the momentum of the water passing beneath. Compare *breastshot*, *overshot* and *pitchback*.

**UNIVALLATE** Of a *hill-fort*: defended by one concentric bank and ditch.

**UPPER CRUCK** A type of timber construction in which curving paired members (*blades*) are supported on a *tie-beam* and rise to the apex [11].

**VAULT** An *arched* stone roof, sometimes imitated in timber, plaster etc. [37]. For the different kinds see *barrel vault, fan-vault, groin-vault, rib-vault, sail vault.*

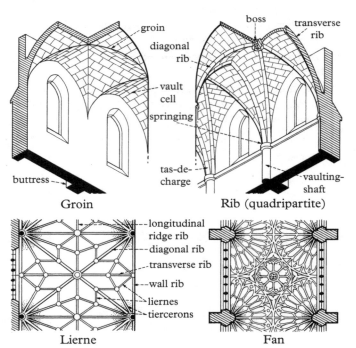

Fig. 37 Vaults

**VAULTING SHAFT**   *Shaft* leading up to the *spring or springing* of a *vault* [37].

**VENETIAN WINDOW**   In *classical* architecture, a window with an arched central *light* flanked by two lower straight-headed ones; the motif is also used for other openings [38]. Also called a *Serlian window*, Serlian motif, Serliana and *Palladian window*.

Fig. 38   Venetian window

**VERMICULATION**   A form of *rustication*, the exaggerated treatment of masonry to give an effect of strength, with a stylized texture like worm-casts [29].

**VERNACULAR**   Refers to buildings using local materials in traditional ways, designed without the intervention of architects. Compare *Neo-vernacular*.

**VESICA**   Oval with pointed ends.

**VICE**   A stair in a circular well with a central supporting *newel*. Also called a *spiral stair* or (Scots) turnpike stair.

**VILLA**   Originally a Roman country house or farm. The term was revived in England in the 18th century under the influence of Palladio (see *Palladian*) and used for smaller, compact country houses. In the later 19th century it was debased to describe any suburban house.

133

**VITRIFIED**   Bricks or tiles fired to a darkened glassy surface.

**VITRUVIAN SCROLL**   *Classical* running ornament of curly waves [39].

Fig. 39   Vitruvian scroll

**VOLUTES**   Spiral scrolls. They occur on *Ionic* capitals [23].
   **ANGLE VOLUTE**: a pair of volutes, turned outwards to meet at the corner of a *capital*.

**VOUSSOIRS**   Wedge-shaped stones forming an *arch* [3].

**WAGON ROOF**  A timber roof with close-set *braces* of polygonal or curved profile, often ceiled between the timbers; also called a *cradle roof*.

**WAINSCOT**  Wooden lining to interior walls, made up of vertical members (*muntins*) and horizontals (*rails*) framing panels; also called *panelling*.

**WALL ARCADE**  In medieval churches, a *blind arcade* forming a *dado* below windows.

**WALL MONUMENT**  A monument attached to the wall and often standing on the floor. Tablets or wall tablets are smaller, with the inscription as the major element.

**WALLHEAD**  (Scots): Straight top of a wall. **WALLHEAD CHIMNEY**: chimney rising from a wallhead [35]. **WALLHEAD GABLE**: *gable* rising from a wallhead.

**WALL-PLATE**  Longitudinal timber on top of a wall, which receives the ends of the *rafters* [34]. Compare *purlin*.

**WALL-POST**  A structural timber set upright in or against a wall.

**WALL-RIB**  A rib set against the wall in a *rib-vault* [37].

**WALL-WALK**  A walk along the *wallhead* of a castle, protected by a *parapet*; also called a parapet walk.

**WARMING ROOM**  Room in an abbey or monastery where a fire burned for comfort.

**WATER WHEELS**  Described by the way water is fed on to the wheel, or by the wheel's structure – a suspension wheel has *wrought iron* or steel spokes like a bicycle wheel. They hold the rim in tension, whilst the older conventional wheel has timber or cast iron spokes which act in compression on the hub. See *breastshot, overshot, pitchback, undershot*. In a water turbine or pelton wheel, water is fed under pressure through a vaned rotor within a casing.

**WATERHOLDING BASE**   Early *Gothic base* with upper and lower *mouldings* separated by a deep hollow.

**WATERLEAF**   A broad tapering leaf shape that turns over at the top, used especially on late 12th-century *capitals* (hence waterleaf capital) and some *classical mouldings* [40].

Fig. 40   Waterleaf capital

**WEALDEN HOUSE**   Type of medieval timber-framed house common in Kent and Sussex, with a central open hall flanked by *bays* of two storeys, roofed in line; the end *bays* are jettied to the front, but the *eaves* are continuous [14].

**WEATHERBOARDING**   Wall *cladding* of overlapping horizontal boards; called *clapboarding* in North America.

**WEATHERING**   Inclined, projecting surface to keep water away from the wall below. Also called *set-off*.

**WEEPERS**   Mourning figures in niches along the sides of some medieval tombs.

**WELL STAIR**   With flights round a square open well framed by *newel posts* [32].

**WHEEL HOUSE**   (Scots): Late *Iron Age* stone dwelling, round with partition walls like wheel spokes.

**WHEEL WINDOW**   A circular window with radiating *shafts* like spokes. Compare *rose window*.

**WIND-BRACES**   Short, usually curved *braces* in a timber-framed roof, connecting *side purlins* or *ridge-piece* with the *principals* [34].

**WINDER**   A step on a curved or turning section of a stair [32].

**WINDER STAIR**   A stair in a rectangular compartment with a central supporting *newel*.

**WRENAISSANCE**   A jocular term for a style of the late 19th and early 20th centuries, based on the works of the English *Baroque* architect Sir Christopher Wren (1632–1723) and his contemporaries. Also called *Neo-Wren*.

**WROUGHT IRON**   Ductile iron that is strong in tension, forged into decorative patterns or forged and rolled into e.g. bars, *joists*, boiler plates. Compare *cast iron*.

**WYATT WINDOW**   Term for the type of large tripartite *sash window* with narrower side *lights* and a segmental *arch* above, made popular by the Wyatt family of architects in the late 18th century.

**WYND**   (Scots): Subsidiary street or lane, often running into a main street.

**YETT** (Scots, *lit.* gate): Hinged openwork gate at a main doorway, made of iron bars alternately penetrating and penetrated [35, 41].

Fig. 41   Yett

**Y-TRACERY**   A form of *bar tracery*, used *c.* 1300, which branches into a Y-shape.

**ZIGZAG**   Used for V-shapes used in series or (later) double series on a *moulding* in *Norman* architecture, especially when on a single plane; also called *chevron*.

# PEVSNER ARCHITECTURAL GUIDES
## VOLUMES IN PRINT

Argyll & Bute: Walker
pub. 2000 / cl / 978-0-300-09670-5

Bath: Forsyth
pub. 2003 / pb / 978-0-300-10177-5

Bedfordshire, Huntingdon & Peterborough: Pevsner
pub. 1968 / cl / 978-0-300-09581-4

Berkshire: Tyack
pub. 2010 / cl / 978-0-300-12662-4

Birmingham: Foster
pub. 2005 / pb / 978-0-300-10731-9

Borders: Cruft, Dunbar & Fawcett
pub. 2006 / cl / 978-0-300-10702-9

Brighton & Hove: Antram & Morrice
pub. 2008 / pb / 978-0-300-12661-7

Bristol: Foyle
pub. 2004 / pb / 978-0-300-10442-4

Buckinghamshire: Pevsner & Williamson
pub. 1994 / cl / 978-0-300-09584-5

Cambridgeshire: Pevsner
pub. 1970 / cl / 978-0-300-09586-9

Carmarthenshire & Ceredigion: Lloyd et al.
pub. 2006 / cl / 978-0-300-10179-9

Cheshire: Pevsner & Hubbard
pub. 1971 / cl / 978-0-300-09588-3

Clwyd: Hubbard
pub. 1986 / cl / 978-0-300-09627-9

Cornwall: Pevsner
pub. 1970 / cl / 978-0-300-09589-0

County Durham: Pevsner & Williamson
pub. 1983 / cl / 978-0-300-09599-9

Cumbria: Hyde
pub. 2010 / cl / 978-0-300-12663-1

Derbyshire: Pevsner
pub. 1978 / cl / 978-0-300-09591-3

Devon: Cherry & Pevsner
pub. 1989 / cl / 978-0-300-09596-8

Dorset: Pevsner & Newman
pub. 1972 / cl / 978-0-300-09598-2

Dublin: Casey
pub. 2005 / cl / 978-0-300-10923-8

Dumfries & Galloway: Gifford
pub. 1996 / cl / 978-0-300-09671-2

Edinburgh: Gifford et al.
pub. 1984 / cl / 978-0-300-09672-9

Essex: Bettley & Pevsner
pub. 2007 / cl / 978-0-300-11614-4

Fife: Gifford
pub. 1988 / cl / 978-0-300-09673-6

Glamorgan: Newman
pub. 1995 / cl / 978-0-300-09629-3

Glasgow: Williamson, Riches & Higgs
pub. 1990 / cl / 978-0-300-09674-3

Gloucestershire 1, the Cotswolds: Verey & Brooks
pub. 1999 / cl / 978-0-300-09604-0

Gloucestershire 2, the Vale & the Forest of Dean:
Verey & Brooks
pub. 2002 / cl / 978-0-300-09733-7

Gwent/Monmouthshire: Newman
pub. 2000 / cl / 978-0-300-09630-9

Gwynedd: Haslam, Orbach & Voelcker
pub. 2009 / cl / 978-0-300-14169-6

Hampshire & the Isle of Wight: Pevsner & Lloyd
pub. 1967 / cl / 978-0-300-09606-4

Hampshire, Winchester & the North: Bullen, Crook,
Hubbock & Pevsner
pub. 2010 / cl / 978-0-300-12084-4

Herefordshire: Pevsner
pub. 1963 / cl / 978-0-300-09609-5

Hertfordshire: Pevsner & Cherry
pub. 1963 / cl / 978-0-300-09611-8

Highland & Islands: Gifford
pub. 1992 / cl / 978-0-300-09625-5

Hull: Neave & Neave
pub. 2010 / pb / 978-0-300-14172-6

Isle of Wight: Lloyd & Pevsner
pub. 2006 / cl / 978-0-300-10733-3

North East & East Kent: Newman
pub. 1983 / cl / 978-0-300-09613-2

West Kent & the Weald: Newman
pub. 1976 / cl / 978-0-300-09614-9

Lancashire, Liverpool and the South West:
Pollard & Pevsner
pub. 2006 / cl / 978-0-300-10910-8

Lancashire, Manchester and the South East:
Hartwell et al.
pub. 2004 / cl / 978-0-300-10583-4

Lancashire, North: Hartwell & Pevsner
pub. 2009 / cl / 978-0-300-12667-9

Leeds: Wrathmell
pub. 2005 / pb / 978-0-300-10736-4

Leicestershire & Rutland: Pevsner & Williamson
pub. 1984 / cl / 978-0-300-09618-7

North Leinster: Casey & Rowan
pub. 1993 / cl / 978-0-300-09668-2

Lincolnshire: Pevsner, Harris & Antram
pub. 1989 / cl / 978-0-300-09620-0

Liverpool: Sharples
pub. 2004 / pb / 978-0-300-10258-1

London 1, the City of London: Bradley & Pevsner
pub. 1997 / cl / 978-0-300-09624-8

London 2, South: Cherry & Pevsner
pub. 1983 / cl / 978-0-300-09651-4

London 3, North West: Cherry & Pevsner
pub. 1991 / cl / 978-0-300-09652-1

London 4, North: Cherry & Pevsner
pub. 1998 / cl / 978-0-300-09653-8

London 5, East: Cherry, O'Brien & Pevsner
pub. 2005 / cl / 978-0-300-10701-2

London 6, Westminster: Bradley & Pevsner
pub. 2003 / cl / 978-0-300-09595-1

London, The City Churches: Bradley & Pevsner
pub. 1998 / pb / 978-0-300-09655-2

Lothian, except Edinburgh: McWilliam
pub. 1978 / cl / 978-0-300-09626-2

Manchester: Hartwell
pub. 2001 / pb / 978-0-300-09666-8

Newcastle & Gateshead: McCombie
pub. 2009 / pb / 978-0-300-12664-8

Norfolk 1, Norwich & North East: Pevsner & Wilson
pub. 1997 / cl / 978-0-300-09607-1

Norfolk 2, North West & South: Pevsner & Wilson
pub. 1999 / cl / 978-0-300-09657-6

Northamptonshire: Pevsner & Cherry
pub. 1973 / cl / 978-0-300-09632-3

Northumberland: Pevsner et al.
pub. 1992 / cl / 978-0-300-09638-5

Nottingham: Harwood
pub. 2008 / pb / 978-0-300-12666-2

Nottinghamshire: Pevsner & Williamson
pub. 1979 / cl / 978-0-300-09636-1

Oxfordshire: Pevsner & Sherwood
pub. 1974 / cl / 978-0-300-09639-2

Pembrokeshire: Lloyd et al.
pub. 2004 / cl / 978-0-300-10178-2

Perth and Kinross: Gifford
pub. 2007 / cl / 978-0-300-10922-1

Powys: Haslam
pub. 1979 / cl / 978-0-300-09631-6

Sheffield: Harman & Minnis
pub. 2004 / pb / 978-0-300-10585-8

Shropshire: Newman & Pevsner
pub. 2006 / cl / 978-0-300-12083-7

North Somerset & Bristol: Pevsner
pub. 1958 / cl / 978-0-300-09640-8

South & West Somerset: Pevsner
pub. 1958 / cl / 978-0-300-09644-6

Staffordshire: Pevsner
pub. 1974 / cl / 978-0-300-09646-0

Stirling & Central Scotland: Gifford & Walker
pub. 2002 / cl / 978-0-300-09594-4

Suffolk: Pevsner & Radcliffe
pub. 1974 / cl / 978-0-300-09648-4

Surrey: Pevsner, Nairn & Cherry
pub. 1971 / cl / 978-0-300-09675-0

Sussex: Pevsner & Nairn
pub. 1965 / cl / 978-0-300-09677-4

North West Ulster: Rowan
pub. 1979 / cl / 978-0-300-09667-5

Warwickshire: Pevsner & Wedgwood
pub. 1966 / cl / 978-0-300-09679-8

Wiltshire: Pevsner & Cherry
pub. 1971 / cl / 978-0-300-09659-0

Worcestershire: Brooks & Pevsner
pub. 2007 / cl / 978-0-300-11298-6

Yorkshire, the North Riding: Pevsner
pub. 1966 / cl / 978-0-300-09665-1

Yorkshire, West Riding: Leach & Pevsner
pub. 2009 / cl / 978-0-300-12665-5

Yorkshire, York & the East Riding: Pevsner & Neave
pub. 1995 / cl / 978-0-300-09593-7